MW01094896

Dear Yoshida,

Congratulations on the publication of your book. I am so happy for you. I met you at the Park Hyatt hotel in Tokyo, where I was a chef, and where you spent four intense and enriching years as a young pastry chef. You were constantly progressing, all the while sharing laughs with the other young cooks, each of them as ambitious as you were. And when I opened my own restaurant, Oakwood, I gave you an important role on the team.

Then you had to return home to take over your father's business. It was not easy at first, but through hard work you overcame difficulties, and your shop became known as the best pâtisserie in all of Shizuoka. Then you said to me, "I am going to live in France in the hopes of opening my own shop." In all honesty, I was very surprised that you wanted to head to France alone after all you had built in Japan. But driven by your curiosity and your energy, you continued to achieve your dreams.

Things must not have been easy when you first arrived. There must have been moments when you wanted to drop everything and return home. But you held on. After overcoming obstacles and working hard to achieve your goal, you opened the Mori Yoshida pâtisserie. What a feat! Even after that accomplishment, you continued to improve your skills by seeking a deeper understanding of French tastes and sensibilities. You worked tirelessly to make the Mori Yoshida pâtisserie what it is today. You have made a place for yourself and become a renowned pastry chef in France—and published your book—through your determination and curiosity, and your personality, which charms everyone you meet.

Changes in Japanese pastry over the last half century owe much to the many Japanese pastry chefs who have created bridges with French culinary culture. With the goal of bringing themselves if only a little bit closer to French tradition, they have gone to considerable efforts to learn the techniques and acquire the knowledge and sensibility of French pastry making. Without this generation of pastry chefs, we would never have seen such an evolution of Western pastry in Japan.

This book presents French pastry as seen through the eyes of a Japanese chef who has thoroughly absorbed the sensibility of this culture. Yoshida, you found a path to freedom in becoming a renowned pastry chef, and you have our full admiration. We will continue to encourage your singular style. Although you appear to have reached the height of your art, you yourself must feel that you are still learning and that you must continue to grow. We will be here, happy to witness your progress, always.

Hideo Yokota

Mori Yoshida

モリヨシダの菓子

Gâteaux

SWEETS

Mori Yoshida

PHOTOGRAPHY BY
CAROLINE FACCIOLI

Gâteaux

TEXT CREATED IN COLLABORATION WITH RYOKO SEKIGUCHI

モリヨシダの菓子

BASED ON AN ORIGINAL IDEA BY JULIE MATHIEU AND MURIEL TALLANDIER

T tra.publishing

PREFACE

The first time a pastry chef writes a book marks a turning point in their life, a kind of culmination. Sharing knowledge through images and recipes is important; it conveys mastery, consistency, and the desire to take one's art further by sharing original creations that have been developed and refined, often over many years.

Mori Yoshida is a man of taste and great humility, whose modesty is matched only by his talent. I met him for the first time in 2018, during the filming of the television show *Le Meilleur Pâtissier—Les Professionnels* ("Best Pastry Chef—Professionals"), where he won the final round, and then again in 2019, when he competed for the title again. I was immediately struck by the quality of his work, in terms of both taste and technique. His creations are incredibly light, harmonious, balanced, and elegant. Throughout the competition, he displayed a considerable calm that commanded respect. As he likes to say, he makes pastry in the French tradition, and adds his personal style—with a particular attention to detail.

Mori is incredibly talented; to taste his pastries is to appreciate his vast knowledge and the meticulousness he brings to each creation. He is one of the rare Japanese pastry chefs to work in and to have opened a shop in Paris, carving out a place for himself among France's pastry elite.

France and its regions are a constant source of inspiration for Mori. In this book, he eagerly shares his advice and the techniques necessary to reproduce his recipes. Whether he is making éclairs, Paris-Brest, Saint-Honoré, or tea cakes and quick breads, each one conveys his constant search for excellence, precision, and an abundance of flavor that gives each pastry a singularity.

It is a privilege and an honor to write the preface to this book, an undisputed celebration of French pastry. And it is a way for me to pay tribute to a perfect and very personal interpretation of this tradition.

Pierre Hermé

FOREWORD

I came to France because I have always admired French pastry, and today I am proud to be recognized as an active participant in this tradition. Sometimes it feels like the world of French pastry is divided, with innovators on one side and craftspeople who uphold tradition on the other. Personally, I try to create things that nourish and ensure that the forms my creations take arise from my explorations into taste.

And I think that it is the act of going to the workshop every day that makes it possible to pass on knowledge. That is how I share my high standard of serving clients products of only the highest quality. I approach being a pastry chef wholeheartedly. Cakes—gâteaux—are mirrors of ourselves. When we make them with sincerity, care, and honesty, what comes out of the oven will have the taste of authenticity. If we try to cheat, to find the easy way, the gâteau will taste artificial.

It would be a shame if professional pastry were only about efficiency. We can create recipes that facilitate the preparation of large quantities or that make pastries easier to store. In contrast, my pastry is demanding: my recipes require skill and experience. But once these have been mastered, the cakes will have finer contours and richer, more nuanced textures.

Perhaps the reason that I, Japanese pastry chef that I am, offer classic French cakes is because I can seem them objectively. I did not spend my childhood looking for Easter eggs or playing with the fève in a galette des rois (king cake). But that is precisely why I do not base myself on any preexisting recipes. I start with a blank slate, asking questions at each step to determine why it is necessary. What matters most to me is that a recipe points the way to a "path of delight."

In this book, I invite you to follow this path using my favorite recipes that correspond to different moments throughout the day.

Mori Yoshida

Table of Contents

64 Boulevard Haussmann, Paris 9th Arrondissement – 8:10 a.m.

CHAP. 1

Morning

Parisian Flan

ACTIVE TIME
45 minutes

RESTING TIME
12 hours + 4 hours

COOKING TIME
1 hour 15 minutes

Although this tart appears simple, it is the most difficult to make, as each step in the recipe can affect the appearance and flavor. I want mine to be perfect, with faultless edges, even when I'm making a hundred of them. That's not to say identical, like products turned out of a factory—but each one should be made with the same fastidiousness.

To our great delight, our French customers love our take on this traditional afternoon snack (although we often sell ours in the morning). It is a simple treat, with nothing superfluous, and a perfect way to start a good day.

Serves 6

EQUIPMENT

1   *12-inch (30-cm) round pastry cutter*
1   *8-inch (20-cm) tart ring, 2½ inches (6 cm) deep*
1   *instant-read thermometer*

—

SHORTCRUST PASTRY

150 G   *unsalted butter, chilled*
300 G   *all-purpose flour (T55)*
12 G   *granulated sugar*
5 G   *fine sea salt*
25 G   *egg yolk (about 1 yolk from 1 large egg)*
60 G   *cold water*

—

CUSTARD FILLING

800 G   *whole milk, divided, at room temperature*
255 G   *heavy cream, divided, at room temperature*
½   *vanilla bean, split lengthwise*
180 G   *superfine sugar*
75 G   *cornstarch*
160 G   *egg yolks (8 yolks from large eggs)*
35 G   *egg whites (about 1½ whites from large eggs)*

Shortcrust pastry

01.   The day before baking, cut the butter into approximately ¼-inch (5-mm) dice. In a large bowl, whisk together the flour, sugar, and salt. Using your fingertips, work in the butter until the mixture resembles coarse crumbs.

02.   Add the egg yolk and water and knead until smooth. Shape into a disk, cover with plastic wrap, and refrigerate overnight.

03.   The next day, on a lightly floured surface, roll the dough to a thickness of about ¼ inch (5 mm). Cut out a 12-inch (30-cm) disk using the pastry cutter. Place the tart ring on a baking sheet lined with parchment paper. Line the ring with the dough: lay the dough over the ring and gently press it into the corners and against the sides. Prick the base of the dough all over with a fork. Place the baking sheet in the refrigerator for at least 1 hour to allow the dough to firm up in the ring.

04.   Preheat the oven to 340°F (170°C). Cut a 12-inch (30-cm) circle of parchment paper and place it over the base of the dough. Top with pie weights. Bake for 30 minutes.

05.   Remove the crust from the oven. Run the blade of a sharp knife along the top edge of the tart ring to trim the crust and obtain a clean edge. Using an oven mitt, remove the pie weights, then remove the parchment paper and return the crust to the oven. Bake for an additional 20 minutes.

Custard filling

01.   Preheat the oven to 340°F (170°C). Combine 725 g of the milk and 180 g of the cream in a large saucepan. Scrape the vanilla bean seeds into the saucepan. Bring to a boil, then turn off the heat. Meanwhile, in a large bowl, whisk together the sugar and cornstarch. Whisk in the egg yolks until well combined.

02.   Whisking vigorously, gradually pour one-third of the hot milk mixture into the egg yolk mixture. Pour back into the saucepan, whisking continuously. Still whisking, cook over medium heat until the custard reaches 172°F (78°C). Remove from the heat and whisk in the remaining 75 g milk and the remaining 75 g cream. Strain the custard through a fine-mesh sieve and pour into the crust.

Baking

01.   Bake at 340°F (170°C) for 20 to 25 minutes. Do not be tempted to remove the ring right away. Let the tart cool for 3 hours at room temperature before removing the ring and serving.

NOTES: I've spent a lot of time pondering what the "essence" of this tart is, and I've concluded that it lies in the balance between the textures of the custard and the crust. In this recipe, the crust is thicker than in standard recipes. By blind-baking the crust before adding the filling, the pastry remains firm for longer. Although this adds an extra step, the attention to detail makes an appreciable difference in taste. Also, because the tart is 2½ inches (6 cm) deep, it can hold more filling than the typical Parisian flan. This makes it easier to appreciate the wonderful contrast between the two consistencies. A blend of milk and cream makes the custard especially silky.

Chocolate Croissants

ACTIVE TIME
45 minutes

RESTING TIME
*3 hours + 12 hours
+ 7 hours*

COOKING TIME
16 minutes

*When I first arrived in France, I'd eat a chocolate croissant every day.
The chocolate—the only ingredient that sets this croissant apart from a regular one—completely
changes the texture. I loved this popular pastry so much that I wanted to create my own version.*

*Today, neighborhood residents stop by our boutique in the mornings to pick up their daily
pain au chocolat. Our regulars include many taxi drivers who take their breaks on our street,
the Avenue de Breteuil. It gives me great pleasure to see the diversity of our customer base, and
it is immensely gratifying to hear them say that they always come for the same thing, because
it proves that the taste is something they never tire of.*

Makes 12

EQUIPMENT

1	*stand mixer*
1	*instant-read thermometer*

—

CROISSANT DOUGH

155 G	*whole milk, at room temperature*
155 G	*water, at room temperature*
22 G	*fresh yeast*
350 G	*pastry flour (T45)*
350 G	*all-purpose flour (T55)*
100 G	*superfine sugar*
14 G	*fine sea salt*
70 G	*invert sugar (Trimoline)*
235 G	*unsalted European-style butter, preferably 84% fat (beurre sec), chilled*
	neutral oil, for greasing bowl

—

CHOCOLATE FILLING

24	*chocolate batons*

—

EGG WASH

50 G	*egg yolks (about 2½ yolks from large eggs)*
5 G	*heavy cream*

Croissant dough

01.   The day before baking, combine the milk and water in a bowl, add the yeast, and stir to dissolve. Fit the stand mixer with the dough hook and place both flours and the sugar, salt, and invert sugar in the bowl. Add the yeast mixture and knead on low speed for 15 minutes. Continue to knead until the dough reaches an internal temperature of 79°F (26°C). Shape the dough into a ball and transfer to a clean bowl lightly greased with the neutral oil. Let rise at room temperature for 3 hours (first rise).

02.   Turn the dough out of the bowl onto a floured work surface and deflate it using the heel of your hand. Once you've released all the air bubbles trapped inside, gather the dough into a ball, place it in a plastic bag, and close the bag. Let rise overnight in the refrigerator (second rise).

Laminating

01.   The next day, using a rolling pin, pound on the butter to flatten it into an 8-inch (20-cm) square.

02.   Remove the dough from the refrigerator and place it on a floured work surface. Flatten the dough again using the heel of your hand to release any air bubbles. As you work, lightly flour the work surface as needed to prevent the dough from sticking. Roll the dough into a 10-inch (25-cm) square. Place the square of butter in the center of the dough at a 45-degree angle, so the corners of the butter touch the sides of the dough. Fold the corners of the dough over the butter so that they meet in the middle, enclosing the butter completely. Pinch the edges together to seal them well.

03.   Roll the dough into a 10 × 14-inch (25 × 35-cm) rectangle and give it a "double turn": fold both of the short ends in so that they meet in the center, then fold the resulting square in half with the seam inside, like a book. Cover the dough with plastic wrap and place it in the freezer for 1 hour.

04.   Repeat step 3: roll the dough into a 10 × 14-inch (25 × 35-cm) rectangle again and give it another double turn. Cover with plastic wrap and return to the freezer for 1 hour. When you remove the dough from the freezer, pound it with the rolling pin to soften it, then roll it into a rectangle of the same size once more and give it one final double turn. Cover with plastic wrap and freeze for 1½ hours.

Shaping and baking

01.   Grease a baking sheet with butter. Roll the dough into a 12½ × 16-inch (32 × 40-cm) rectangle, about ¼ inch (5 mm) thick. Cut into twelve approximately 3 × 5-inch (8 × 13-cm) rectangles (each should weigh about 3 oz./90 g). Place 2 chocolate batons on one short end of each, ¾ inch (2 cm) from the edge. Roll up the dough around the chocolate batons to enclose them. Place the shaped croissants on the prepared baking sheet and place in an unheated oven with a bowl of warm water (approximately 86°F/30°C) inside to keep the air moist and encourage the dough to rise. Close the oven door and let the croissants rise for 3 to 4 hours, until approximately doubled in size.

02.   Remove the croissants and bowl of water from the oven and preheat the oven to 340°F (170°C). To prepare the egg wash, whisk together the egg yolk and cream. Brush over the croissants and bake for 16 minutes.

NOTES: Don't be tempted to skip the chilling step between rounds of folding—it will really improve the final result.

Croissants

ACTIVE TIME	RESTING TIME	COOKING TIME
45 minutes	3 hours + 12 hours + 7 hours	16 minutes

I developed a passion for the process of fermentation when I arrived in France—so much so that one day, while working at La Pâtisserie des Rêves, I took some kouign amann dough home with me to observe its evolution. Although I got a good scolding, watching the dough attentively helped me to understand leavening in all its complexity. Success depends not only on the type of flour and yeast but also on the room temperature and ambient humidity.

You must watch the dough closely and adjust the amount of water and proofing (or rising) time as needed, based on what you see. Paying attention leads to perfection, although this is easier said than done. I've been making croissant dough for about twenty years now, and I've only recently begun to grasp all the intricacies.

Makes 12

EQUIPMENT

1	*stand mixer*
1	*instant-read thermometer*

—

CROISSANT DOUGH

155 G	*whole milk, at room temperature*
155 G	*water, at room temperature*
22 G	*fresh yeast*
350 G	*pastry flour (T45)*
350 G	*all-purpose flour (T55)*
98 G	*superfine sugar*
14 G	*fine sea salt*
70 G	*invert sugar (Trimoline)*
233 G	*unsalted European-style butter, preferably 84% fat (beurre sec), chilled*
	neutral oil, for greasing bowl

—

EGG WASH

60 G	*egg yolks (about 3 yolks from large eggs)*
6 G	*heavy cream*

Croissant dough

01.   The day before baking, combine the milk and water in a bowl. Crumble in the yeast, and stir to dissolve. Fit the stand mixer with the dough hook and place both flours and the sugar, salt, and invert sugar in the bowl. Add the yeast mixture and knead on low speed for 15 minutes. Continue to knead until the dough reaches an internal temperature of 79°F (26°C). Shape the dough into a ball and transfer to a clean bowl lightly greased with the neutral oil. Let rise at room temperature for 3 hours (first rise).

02.   Turn the dough out of the bowl onto a floured work surface and deflate it using the heel of your hand. Once you've released all the air bubbles trapped inside, gather the dough into a ball, place it in a plastic bag, and close the bag. Let rise overnight in the refrigerator (second rise).

Laminating

01.   The next day, using a rolling pin, pound on the butter to flatten it into an 8-inch (20-cm) square.

02.   Remove the dough from the refrigerator and place it on a floured work surface. Flatten the dough again using the heel of your hand to release any air bubbles. As you work, lightly flour the work surface as needed to prevent the dough from sticking. Roll the dough into a 10-inch (25-cm) square. Place the square of butter in the center of the dough at a 45-degree angle, so the corners of the butter touch the sides of the dough. Fold the corners of the dough over the butter so that they meet in the middle, enclosing the butter completely. Pinch the edges together to seal them well.

03.   Roll the dough into a 10 × 14-inch (25 × 35-cm) rectangle and give it a "double turn": fold both of the short ends in so that they meet in the center, then fold the resulting square in half with the seam inside, like a book. Cover the dough with plastic wrap and place it in the freezer for 1 hour.

Shaping and baking

01.   Grease a baking sheet with butter. Roll the dough into an 8½ × 16-inch (22 × 40-cm) rectangle, about ¼ inch (5 mm) thick. Cut into twelve isosceles triangles measuring approximately 4½ inches (11 cm) at the base and 8 inches (20 cm) tall (each should weigh about 3 oz./90 g). Starting at the base, roll each triangle up toward the tip. Place the shaped croissants on the prepared baking sheet with the tips underneath. Place in an unheated oven with a bowl of warm water (approximately 86°F/30°C) inside to keep the air moist and encourage the dough to rise. Close the oven door and let the croissants rise for 3 to 4 hours, until approximately doubled in size.

02.   Remove the croissants and bowl of water from the oven and preheat the oven to 340°F (170°C). To prepare the egg wash, whisk together the egg yolk and cream. Brush over the croissants and bake for 16 minutes.

Brioche Nanterre

ACTIVE TIME	RESTING TIME	COOKING TIME
30 minutes	*13 hours + 3 hours*	*20 minutes*

Many French cakes are made with brioche dough, including galettes des rois (king cakes) and pain perdu (French toast). That is why I wanted to perfect the recipe, which lends itself to so many variations and plays such an important role in daily life in France.

In our boutique, I've noticed that brioche enthusiasts and croissant lovers are not necessarily one and the same. Working in France has allowed me to learn more about the habits of some of the world's top brioche consumers.

Makes 3

EQUIPMENT

1	*stand mixer*
3	*7 × 6½ × 2¾-inch (18 × 16 × 7-cm) loaf pans*

—

BRIOCHE DOUGH

365 G	*all-purpose flour (T55)*
40 G	*superfine sugar*
8 G	*fine sea salt*
35 G	*whole milk, at room temperature*
14 G	*fresh yeast*
180 G	*lightly beaten eggs (about 3½ large eggs)*
35 G	*egg yolks (about 2 yolks from large eggs)*
180 G	*unsalted butter, at room temperature*

—

EGG WASH

30 G	*egg yolks (about 1½ yolks from large eggs)*
3 G	*heavy cream*

Brioche dough

01. The day before baking, fit the stand mixer with the dough hook and place the flour, sugar, and salt in the bowl. Pour the milk into a small bowl, crumble in the yeast, and stir to dissolve. Add to the mixer bowl. In a separate bowl, whisk together the eggs and egg yolks. Pour one-third of the egg mixture into the mixer bowl. Knead on medium speed until the gluten is well developed and passes the "windowpane" test: gently stretch a little dough. If it stretches until thin and translucent without tearing, it's ready; if not, keep kneading.

02. With the mixer still running on medium speed, gradually add the remaining egg mixture. Continue kneading until the dough is smooth and pulls away from the sides of the bowl. Add one-third of the butter at a time, waiting until it is fully incorporated before continuing.

03. Once all the butter is incorporated and the dough is smooth and elastic, shape the dough into a ball and place it in a clean bowl. Cover the bowl with plastic wrap and let it rise in the refrigerator for 1 hour (first rise).

04. Turn the dough out of the bowl onto a lightly floured work surface and deflate it using the heel of your hand. Once you've released all the air bubbles trapped inside, gather the dough into a ball, place it in a plastic bag, and close the bag. Let rise overnight in the refrigerator (second rise).

Shaping and baking

01. The next day, grease the loaf pans with butter. Remove the dough from the refrigerator and place it on a floured work surface. Flatten the dough again using the heel of your hand to release any air bubbles. Divide the dough into twelve pieces weighing 70 g each and shape each piece into a ball. Place four balls of dough in each prepared loaf pan, seam-side down and lined up carefully.

02. Cover the pans with a damp dish towel and place them in a warm place 82°F (28°C). Let the dough rise for 2½ to 3 hours (third rise), keeping an eye on it. Remove the towel as soon as the dough touches it.

03. Meanwhile, preheat the oven to 340°F (170°C). To prepare the egg wash, whisk together the egg yolk and cream. Brush over the dough. Using scissors, cut lengthwise slits into the tops of the dough. Place pans in the oven, leaving a little space between them, and bake for 20 minutes.

04. Immediately remove the brioches from their pans: place a clean dish towel on a work surface, turn the pans upside down, and tap on the bases to release the brioche. Transfer to a rack and let cool completely.

NOTES: Rich in eggs and butter, this recipe yields light, airy loaves. The characteristics of the eggs are among the many factors that influence the quality of leavened dough. Their texture and flavor vary with the seasons, even if they are sourced from the same producer.

As pastry chefs, we know summer has arrived just by looking at the eggs. Therein lies the difficulty, but also all the pleasure, of making egg-based doughs.

Puff-Pastry Brioche

ACTIVE TIME	RESTING TIME	COOKING TIME
30 minutes	*13 hours + 3 hours*	*25 minutes*

I first tried this puff-pastry brioche while doing a stage with Guy Savoy, who had the idea of using flaky brioche in haute cuisine. Savoy's ultra-luxe version piqued my curiosity, and I wanted to make my own.

I had never made it myself, either at Guy Savoy's restaurant or at La Pâtisserie des Rêves, so I had to find the right proportions of flour and butter on my own. One day, I tried making puff-pastry brioche with the same dough as the Brioche Nanterre. I'd found the answer.

Makes 3

EQUIPMENT

1	*stand mixer*
3	*7 × 6½ × 2¾-inch (18 × 16 × 7-cm) loaf pans*

—

BRIOCHE DOUGH

365 G	*all-purpose flour (T55)*
40 G	*superfine sugar*
8 G	*fine sea salt*
35 G	*whole milk*
14 G	*fresh yeast*
180 G	*lightly beaten eggs (about 3½ large eggs)*
35 G	*egg yolks (about 2 yolks from large eggs)*
180 G	*unsalted butter, at room temperature*

—

PUFF-PASTRY BRIOCHE

670 G	*brioche dough (SEE ABOVE)*
200 G	*unsalted European-style butter, preferably 84% fat (beurre sec), chilled*

Brioche dough

01.   The day before baking, fit the stand mixer with the dough hook and place the flour, sugar, and salt in the bowl. Pour the milk into a bowl, crumble in the yeast, and stir to dissolve. Add to the mixer bowl. In a separate bowl, whisk together the eggs and egg yolks. Pour one-third of the egg mixture into the mixer bowl. Knead on medium speed until the gluten is well developed and passes the "windowpane" test: gently stretch a little dough. If it stretches until thin and translucent without tearing, it's ready; if not, keep kneading. With the mixer still running on medium speed, gradually add the remaining egg mixture. Continue kneading until the dough is smooth and pulls away from the sides of the bowl. Add one-third of the butter at a time, waiting until it is fully incorporated before continuing.

02.   Once all the butter is incorporated and the dough is smooth and elastic, shape the dough into a ball and place it in a clean bowl. Cover the bowl with plastic wrap and let it rise in the refrigerator for 1 hour (first rise).

03.   Turn the dough out of the bowl onto a lightly floured work surface and deflate it using the heel of your hand. Once you've released all the air bubbles trapped inside, shape the dough into an 8-inch (20-cm) square, cover it with plastic wrap, and let it rise overnight in the refrigerator (second rise).

Puff-pastry brioche

01.   The next day, using a rolling pin, pound on the butter to flatten it into a 6-inch (15-cm) square.

02.   Remove the dough square from the refrigerator and reshape it into an 8-inch (20-cm) square if necessary. Place the square of butter in the center of the dough square at a 45-degree angle, so the corners of the butter touch the sides of the dough. Fold the corners of the dough over the butter so that they meet in the middle, enclosing the butter completely. Pinch the edges together to seal them well.

03.   Roll the dough into a 10 × 17¾-inch (25 × 45-cm) rectangle and give it a "double turn": fold both of the short ends in so that they meet in the center, then fold the resulting square in half with the seam inside, like a book. Cover the dough with plastic wrap and place it in the freezer for 30 minutes.

04.   Repeat step 3: roll the dough into a 10 × 17¾-inch (25 × 45-cm) rectangle again and give it another double turn. Cover with plastic wrap and return to the freezer for 30 minutes. When you remove the dough from the freezer, pound it with the rolling pin to soften it.

05.   Roll the dough once more into a rectangle of the same size once more and give it one final double turn. Cover with plastic wrap and freeze for another 30 minutes. Roll the dough one final time into a 10 × 17¾-inch (25 × 45-cm) rectangle, about ¼ inch (5 mm) thick. Roll up the dough tightly and place it in the freezer once more for 30 minutes. Trim the ends of the roll, then cut the roll into twelve slices, about 1½ inches (3.5) cm wide and 65 g each.

Baking

01.   Grease the loaf pans with butter and place four slices of dough in each, with the cut side facing up. Cover the pans with a damp dish towel and place them in a warm place (82°F/28°C). Let the dough rise for 2½ to 3 hours (second rise), keeping an eye on it. Remove the towel as soon as the dough fills the pans two-thirds of the way.

02.   Meanwhile, preheat the oven to 340°F (170°C). Place the pans in the oven and cover them with a baking sheet to prevent them from rising too much (see notes). Bake for 25 minutes.

03.   Immediately remove the brioches from their pans: place a clean dish towel on a work surface, turn the pans upside down, and tap on the bases to release the brioche. Transfer to a rack and let cool completely.

NOTES: It is essential to cover the pans well while this puff-pastry brioche bakes. Otherwise, the dough will rise too much, creating holes inside the brioche, and the crust will become too crisp.

It is also important to allow the brioche to cool completely before slicing, as this ensures a uniform texture throughout

Citrus Marmalade

ACTIVE TIME
45 minutes

RESTING TIME
3 hours + 24 hours

COOKING TIME
20 minutes

*I was already familiar with the fruits used in this recipe before I arrived in France.
Yet I was still amazed by the varieties grown on the French island of Corsica, which offer an incredible palette
of colors. I have used citrus in many ways: there are endless possibilities, and each cake can have its own unique
nuances. This is freedom: the chance to taste and create combinations that suit your preferences.*

*This marmalade is an attempt to capture my vision of citrus by combining several different fruits.
However, it is complicated to make, as these fruits do not all grow in the same season.*

Makes 5 jars

EQUIPMENT

1	*refractometer (optional)*
5	*(1¼-cup/300-ml) jars*

—

CONFITURE

400 G	*oranges (2 oranges)*
380 G	*grapefruit (1 grapefruit)*
120 G	*lemon (1 lemon)*
120 G	*lime (1 lime)*
1.5 L	*water*
820 G	*demerara sugar*
400 G	*orange juice*
15 G	*superfine sugar*
3 G	*pectin NH*

Preparing the fruit

01.   The day before making the marmalade, wash the oranges, grapefruit, lemon, and lime under hot water to remove any wax coating. Cut the ends off the oranges, then cut each orange into eight equal wedges, removing the central white part. Cut each wedge crosswise into approximately ¼-inch (5-mm) slices.

02.   Using a vegetable peeler, peel off the outer layer of the grapefruit. Cut the peel into strips approximately ¼ inch (5 mm) wide. Using a sharp knife, cut the white pith off the fruit. Cut the peeled grapefruit into eight equal wedges, then cut each wedge crosswise into approximately ½-inch (1-cm) pieces.

03.   Cut the ends off the lemon and lime and cut each into eight equal wedges. Separate the fruit from the peels. Cut the peels into strips approximately ¼ inch (5 mm) wide, then cut the fruit into ½-inch (1-cm) pieces.

Cooking

01.   In a large saucepan, bring the water to a boil. Add the grapefruit, lemon, and lime peels. Return to a boil, then cook over medium heat for 10 minutes to temper the bitterness. Drain the peels in a fine-mesh sieve, then place them in a large bowl. Add the cut fruit pieces and the demerara sugar and stir to blend. Let sit at room temperature for 3 hours.

02.   Transfer the fruit-sugar mixture to a large saucepan, add the orange juice, and bring to a boil. As soon as the first bubbles appear, remove the pan from the heat. Let cool to room temperature, then let macerate overnight in the refrigerator.

03.   The next day, combine the superfine sugar and pectin in a small bowl. Remove the saucepan from the refrigerator and bring the marmalade mixture to a boil. Foam will rise to the surface early in the cooking process; be sure to skim it off as soon as it appears. If you have a refractometer, use it to check the sugar content. Continue to cook until the mixture reaches 55° Brix, then stir in the pectin and sugar. Stirring continuously, cook over medium heat for 1 minute to activate the pectin, allowing it to set. (If you do not have a refractometer, let the mixture cook at a boil for 10 minutes before adding the pectin and sugar.)

Canning

01.   Using a small ladle, fill the jars to just shy of the brim with the marmalade and screw the lids on tightly. Place them upside down in a large pot and pour in enough water to cover them by two-thirds. Bring the water to a boil, then reduce the heat to low and cook for an additional 10 minutes. This pasteurizes the marmalade.

02.   Remove the jars from the water and rinse them under a gentle stream of cold water.

NOTES: With this recipe, I wanted to convey the refreshing sensation of biting directly into the fruit. To achieve this, I reduce the sugar content by leaving large pieces of zest. Be sure to remove enough bitterness from the grapefruit peel, boiling it for longer if necessary.

Banana Turnovers

ACTIVE TIME	RESTING TIME	COOKING TIME
1 hour	*3 hours*	*40 minutes*

*In Japan, it is hard to find good apple turnovers because the humidity makes the puff pastry turn soft.
In France, the texture is enjoyable, but the filling is often too sweet. The first turnover that truly impressed me
was from a Parisian bakery; the texture and flavor were perfectly balanced. Later, I came across lemon
and black currant versions at a different bakery, and that inspired me to create my own.*

*So I invented this banana turnover.
The French are used to apple turnovers—I wanted to introduce them to the world of banana cakes,
often neglected in haute pâtisserie. To my surprise, this turnover took off even faster than the banana bread
I also sell in my boutique.*

Makes 8

EQUIPMENT

1	*6-inch (15-cm) round pastry cutter*
600 G	*pastry bag*

—

BANANA COMPOTE

35 G	*superfine sugar*
25 G	*unsalted butter, at room temperature*
370 G	*peeled ripe bananas (about 3 medium bananas, see notes), cut into 1 ¼-inch (3-cm) pieces*
	Finely grated orange zest

—

600 G	*inverse puff pastry* (P. 172)

—

ASSEMBLY

1	*lightly beaten egg white demerara sugar, for sprinkling*

Banana compote

01.   In a large heavy saucepan, heat the sugar until it melts and caramelizes. As soon as small bubbles appear on the surface and the caramel is a rich golden color, remove the pan from the heat and add the butter to stop the cooking. Stir until smooth.

02.   Add the bananas to the saucepan and place over medium heat. Cook, stirring, for about 5 minutes, until the mixture thickens and bubbles.

03.   Remove from the heat and stir in orange zest to taste, then pour the mixture into a bowl and let cool. Transfer to the pastry bag.

Assembling and baking

SEE THE STEP-BY-STEP INSTRUCTIONS ON PAGES 30–31.

→

NOTES: For these turnovers and the other banana recipes, use bananas with black spots on the skin. These spots are a sign of ripeness and sugar. The fruit will be softer and less fibrous, which will give the compote a wonderful melt-in-the-mouth consistency.

The orange zest and caramel make the banana flavor especially decadent.

Once the pastry has been rolled out, it tends to shrink back towards the center, especially when baked. I take advantage of this reaction to give the turnover a banana-like shape. That is why it is important to keep the pastry in the same direction it was rolled out when assembling the turnovers.

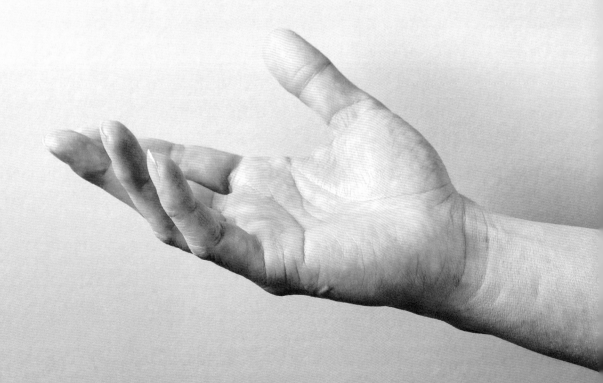

Step-by-Step

ASSEMBLING THE BANANA TURNOVERS

01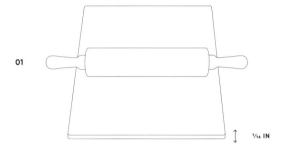

Roll the pastry to a thickness of about ¹⁄₁₆ inch (2 mm).

02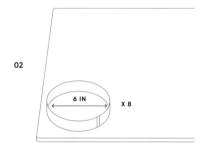

Using the pastry cutter, cut out eight 6-inch (15-cm) disks. For the following three steps, keep the dough facing the same way it was rolled out, without rotating it. This will ensure it has the desired shape after baking (see notes).

03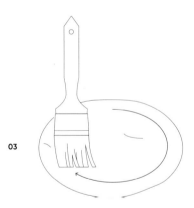

Brush a thin layer of egg white around the edges of the dough disks.

04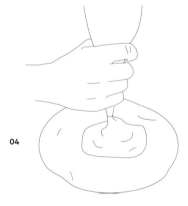

Pipe 50 g of banana compote into the center of each.

05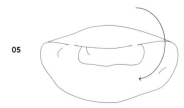

Fold the dough in half over the compote, gently pressing down to release any air.

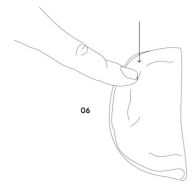

06

Press down on the edges to seal them well.

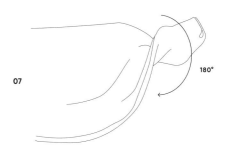

07

180°

Take one corner of each turnover and twist it around 180 degrees. Place the shaped turnovers on a baking sheet and let rest in the refrigerator for 3 hours.

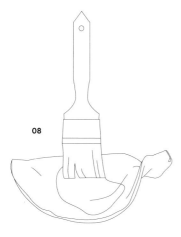

08

Preheat the oven to 340°F (170°C).
Brush a thin layer of water over the tops of the turnovers.

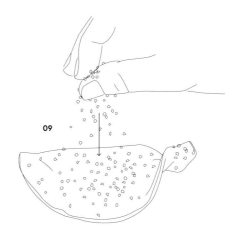

09

Sprinkle generously with demerara sugar.

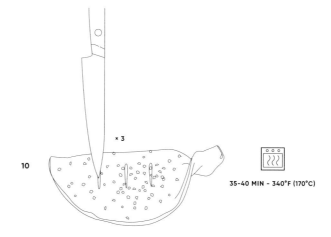

10

× 3

35-40 MIN - 340°F (170°C)

With the tip of a paring knife, cut three slits into the top of each turnover.
Bake for 35 to 40 minutes. Let cool.

Banana Bread

ACTIVE TIME
30 minutes

COOKING TIME
40 minutes

While working in a hotel in Japan run by an American hotel group, I became familiar with different kinds of banana cakes and pastries, especially banana bread.

*With its sweet taste and tender crumb, banana bread is a treat at any time of day.
It is also energizing and filling, making it perfect for breakfast.
To make the banana flavor even more prominent, I developed this recipe,
which contains more fruit than traditional banana bread.*

Makes 3 loaves

EQUIPMENT

3	*7 × 6½ × 2¾-inch (18 × 16 × 7-cm) loaf pans*

—

BANANA BREAD

75 G	*unsalted butter, at room temperature*
130 G	*demerara sugar*
3 G	*fine sea salt*
160 G	*lightly beaten eggs (about 3 large eggs)*
130 G	*pastry flour (T45)*
130 G	*all-purpose flour (T55)*
6 G	*baking soda*
510 G	*peeled ripe bananas (about 5 medium bananas, see notes)*
65 G	*wildflower honey (miel toutes fleurs)*
65 G	*walnut halves*

Banana bread

01.   Preheat the oven to 350°F (180°C) and line the loaf pans with parchment paper.

02.   In a large bowl, stir together the butter, sugar, and salt. Stir in half of the eggs until well incorporated, then stir in the remaining eggs.

03.   Sift both flours into a separate bowl, then whisk in the baking soda. Stir into the butter-egg mixture just until well combined.

04.   Mash the bananas in a separate bowl using your hands or a fork, then stir them into the batter, along with the honey and walnut halves.

05.   Divide the batter between the three pans.

06.   Place the pans in the oven and bake for 40 minutes.

07.   Let the loaves cool in the pans for 15 minutes, then remove them with the parchment paper. Wait until they have cooled completely before removing the paper.

NOTES: This is a relatively easy recipe. The key is to use plenty of bananas to enhance the flavor and to choose bananas that are ripe with black spots on the peel. Because the batter is mixed by hand, there may be small pieces of fruit in it, but that's okay—they add interesting texture to the bread.

Madeleines

ACTIVE TIME
20 minutes

RESTING TIME
12 hours

COOKING TIME
12 minutes

Two of my French customers—a couple—come in every two weeks to order thirty madeleines. My madeleines are not necessarily original, but my customers' loyalty has made me consider the essence of this delicacy: the flavor, texture, and how perfectly it pairs with coffee or tea.

I've reached the conclusion that, once again, it's the little details that make all the difference.

Makes 24

EQUIPMENT

2	*12-cavity madeleine pans (or use one 24-cavity pan)*
1	*pastry bag*
1	*⅓-inch (9-mm) plain tip*
1	*instant-read thermometer*

—

BATTER

150 G	*lightly beaten eggs (3 large eggs)*
180 G	*confectioners' sugar*
120 G	*pastry flour (T45)*
30 G	*almond flour*
5 G	*baking powder*
150 G	*unsalted butter, heated to about 104°F (40°C)*
	grated zest of ½ lemon

—

FOR THE PANS

unsalted butter, at room temperature
flour

Madeleine batter

01.   The day before baking, whisk together the eggs and confectioners' sugar in a large bowl set over a 104°F (40°C) water bath, until pale and thick.

02.   Sift the pastry flour, almond flour, and baking powder together into a bowl, then stir them into the egg mixture.

03.   Add the butter and lemon zest and stir until well combined and smooth.

04.   Press plastic wrap over the surface of the batter and let rest overnight in the refrigerator.

Baking

01.   The next day, preheat the oven to 400°F (200°C). Carefully grease the madeleine pans with butter and dust with flour.

02.   Spoon the madeleine batter into the pastry bag fitted with the ⅓-inch (9-mm) tip and pipe into the pans, filling each cavity two-thirds full. Bake for 10 to 12 minutes, until domed and golden.

03.   Immediately turn the mold upside down and gently tap the edge of the pan on the work surface or counter to release the madeleines.

NOTES: Madeleines are proof that each step in the recipe matters. Some people think you can simplify the steps, but the results don't taste the same. Every detail counts: letting the dough rest overnight after adding the lemon zest to mellow the flavor, coating the pan well with butter, and dusting it with flour.

Japanese Crème Caramel

ACTIVE TIME
30 minutes

RESTING TIME
3 hours

COOKING TIME
40 minutes

My version of crème caramel has an especially silky, velvety texture because it contains sweetened condensed milk and extra egg yolks. It resembles the crème caramel found in Japan.

I'm sure it will appeal to everyone, not just the Japanese.
It is quite different from what the French know, but every crème caramel, whether French or Japanese, has its own charm.

Makes 6 jars

EQUIPMENT

6	*5¼-ounce (156-ml) glass jars*
1	*instant-read thermometer*

—

DRY CARAMEL

200 G	*superfine sugar*

—

CUSTARD

355 G	*whole milk*
35 G	*superfine sugar*
40 G	*egg yolks (about 2 yolks from large eggs)*
40 G	*lightly beaten eggs (about 1 large egg)*
40 G	*sweetened condensed milk*

Dry caramel

01.   Line a baking sheet with parchment paper. In a small heavy saucepan, heat the sugar until it melts and begins to caramelize. Gently swirl the pan. As soon as fine bubbles appear on the surface, turn off the heat and continue to swirl the pan for 10 seconds. The caramel will continue to darken into a rich golden color (see notes). Pour the caramel onto the parchment-lined baking sheet and leave it to cool and harden. Break the caramel into pieces and place about 6 g in each jar.

Custard

01.   Preheat the oven to 300°F (150°C). Combine the milk and sugar in a saucepan and warm to 140°F (60°C). In a large bowl, whisk together the egg yolks, lightly beaten eggs, and sweetened condensed milk. Whisking continuously, gradually pour in the hot milk-sugar mixture. Use a ladle to scoop off any foam that forms on the surface, and discard.

02.   Pour 80 g of custard into each jar, over the caramel pieces. Place the jars in a Dutch oven and pour in enough water to come up to the top of the custard. Cover the Dutch oven and bake for 35 to 40 minutes, just until the custard centers are just set (see notes).

03.   Remove the jars from the hot water and immediately cover them with plastic wrap to prevent the custard from drying out. Let cool to room temperature, then chill for at least 3 hours before serving.

NOTES: Cooking the caramel until it is as dark as possible without burning it will enhance the flavor contrast.

It is very important to remove the crème caramel from the oven as soon as the center of the custard starts to set. Carefully pick up one jar and shake it gently; if the center seems firm but the outside remains a bit looser, the crème caramel is done. If it continues to bake, it will become too firm.

Covering the Dutch oven with the lid ensures even cooking, resulting in a smoother texture.

Finally, to ensure the cream cooks properly, use glass or ceramic jars.

Luxembourg Garden, Paris 6th Arrondissement –11:34 a.m.

CHAP. 2

11 a.m.

Nectarine Tartlets

ACTIVE TIME
30 minutes

COOKING TIME
25 minutes

*I first discovered this fruit while shopping at a Paris market.
When I tasted it, I found that it was firmer than a peach and had the perfect degree
of acidity—even the skin was delicious!*

*That was when it occurred to me to cook nectarines, to achieve a balance of sweetness
and acidity, and to create this tart. It seems to me that nectarines are rarely eaten
cooked in France, and yet they are delicious when prepared that way.*

Makes 6

EQUIPMENT

1   *4 ¼-inch (11-cm) round
     pastry cutter*
1   *pastry bag*
1   *¹⁄₁₆-inch (1-mm) plain tip*
1   *spray bottle of water*

—

TARTLETS

240 G   *inverse puff pastry* (P. 172)
60 G   *almond cream* (P. 177)
         superfine sugar
3   *yellow nectarines*

—

DECORATION

         apricot glaze

Assembly and baking

01.   Preheat the oven to 340°F (170°C). Line a baking sheet with parchment paper. Roll the pastry to a thickness of about ¹⁄₁₆ inch (2 mm). Prick the base of the dough all over with a fork. Cut out six 4 ¼-inch (11-cm) disks with the pastry cutter. Fit the pastry bag with the ¹⁄₁₆-inch (1-mm) tip and fill with the almond cream. Pipe 10 g of almond cream in the center of each tart shell, to a diameter of about 2 inches (5 cm).

02.   Fill the base of a shallow, wide bowl with superfine sugar. Using the spray bottle, moisten the bottoms and edges of the tartlet shells. Dip the shells in the sugar to coat the bottoms, then sprinkle sugar on the edges.

03.   Cut the nectarines in half, then into slices about ½ inch (1 cm) thick (about ten per nectarine). Arrange 3 nectarine slices in a circle around the almond cream in each shell, skin facing out, leaving ½ inch (1 cm) of pastry exposed. Place 2 nectarine slices in the center of the pastry, on top of the almond cream.

04.   Place the tartlets on the baking sheet and bake for 25 minutes, until the bottoms are caramelized and the edges a deep golden brown.

05.   While the tartlets are still warm, brush each one with a thin layer of apricot glaze.

NOTES: You can also use white nectarines for this recipe.

Don't skip sugaring the puff pastry—it is essential to achieving a crunchy texture.

Vertige

ACTIVE TIME	RESTING TIME	COOKING TIME
30 minutes	*12 hours + 4 hours 30 minutes*	*25 minutes*

*Chocolate, lime zest, and green cardamom are a beautiful marriage. My original idea was
to create a chocolate terrine using Peruvian chocolate, which has a powerful aroma.
Then, after several iterations, I added lime, which has a fresh, tart, sharp flavor. But I was still
not satisfied; I wanted to find a flavor that would linger a little longer on the palate.*

*Then one day while preparing curry at home, I realized that green cardamom, with its citrus-like notes,
could counterbalance the richness of chocolate. I named this cake for its ever-evolving combination
of flavors; in each bite, you'll experience new aromas and tastes.*

Serves 6

EQUIPMENT

1	*instant-read thermometer*
1	*6 × 7 × 2 ¾-inch (16 × 18 × 7-cm) rectangular cake pan*

—

BATTER

125 G	*lightly beaten eggs (about 2 ½ large eggs)*
	finely grated zest of ½ lime
	½ green cardamom pod, crushed in a mortar and pestle
165 G	*Valrhona Andoa Noire dark chocolate, 70% cacao, chopped*
125 G	*unsalted butter*
75 G	*superfine sugar*

—

DECORATION

	cocoa powder

Batter

01.　The day before baking, place the eggs, lime zest, and crushed cardamom pod in a medium bowl and gently combine. Cover with plastic wrap and let rest in the refrigerator overnight (see notes).

Assembly and baking

01.　The next day, preheat the oven to 325°F (160°C). Place the chocolate and butter in a small bowl set over a saucepan of barely simmering water. Stir to melt, and heat until the mixture reaches 122°F (50°C).

02.　Remove the egg mixture from the refrigerator and stir in the sugar. Set the bowl over a saucepan of barely simmering water and heat, stirring, until the mixture reaches 122°F (50°C). While it is still hot, strain it through a fine-mesh sieve into the bowl with the chocolate. Whisk until smooth.

03.　Line the cake pan with parchment paper and pour in 450 g of the batter. Place the cake pan in a larger baking dish and pour in enough hot water to come halfway up the sides of the pan. Bake for 25 minutes.

04.　Remove the pan from the baking dish and let cool at room temperature for 30 minutes, then chill in the refrigerator for 3–4 hours.

Decoration

01.　Turn the cake out of the pan. Using a fine-mesh sieve, dust the cake with cocoa powder.

NOTES: The overnight rest for the eggs, lime zest, and cardamom is necessary to infuse the eggs with flavor.

Apricot Tartlets

ACTIVE TIME	RESTING TIME	COOKING TIME
1 hour	*5 hours*	*45 minutes*

*Because apricot season is so brief, it is difficult to make desserts with the fruit.
It took me four years to perfect a recipe that delivers the sensation of biting into a fresh
apricot and the feeling of early summer.*

*The fruit's pleasant acidity is showcased by the apricot compote, enhanced with lemon,
and by the baked apricots. Both the apricot's flavor and freshness are palpable.*

Makes 6

EQUIPMENT

1	*immersion blender*
1	*Silikomart SF013 silicone tartlet mold (2 ½ inches at the base, 2 ¾ inches at the rim, ½ inch tall (6 × 7 × 1.5 cm)*
1	*4 ¼-inch (11-cm) round pastry cutter*
6	*3 ¼-inch (8-cm) tart rings, ½ inch (1.5 cm) deep*
	pie weights
1	*pastry bag*
1	*plain round tip*

—

ROASTED APRICOTS

3	*apricots, halved and pitted*

—

APRICOT COMPOTE

1 G	*gelatin powder*
5 G	*water, heated to 122°F (50°C)*
535 G	*pitted apricots, halved*
150 G	*superfine sugar, divided*
25 G	*freshly squeezed lemon juice*
4 G	*pectin NH*

—

ASSEMBLY AND DECORATION

480 G	*inverse puff pastry (P. 172)*
480 G	*pastry cream (P. 170)*
	snow sugar (non-melting sugar)
	neutral mirror glaze

Roasted apricots

01.   Preheat the oven to 325°F (160°C).

02.   Line a baking sheet with parchment paper. Arrange each apricot half cut-side down on the baking sheet. Bake for 15 minutes. Remove from oven and set aside.

Apricot compote

01.   In a small bowl, dissolve the gelatin powder in the 122°F (50°C) water.

02.   Place the apricot halves, 135 g of the sugar, and the lemon juice in a saucepan and bring to a boil over low heat. Cook, stirring occasionally, until the apricots soften into a compote.

03.   In a small bowl, combine the pectin and the remaining 15 g sugar. Add this mixture to the saucepan and cook until the pectin activates and thickens the compote.

04.   Stir in the dissolved gelatin. With the immersion blender, blend the compote to break up any large pieces.

05.   Place a roasted apricot half cut-side up in each tartlet mold and fill with compote. Place in the freezer for 3 hours.

Tartlet shells and assembly

SEE THE STEP-BY-STEP INSTRUCTIONS ON PAGES 46–47.

NOTES: Apricots can have varying degrees of sweetness and acidity, so you must be careful to balance the flavors in your tart depending on the fruit you find. Be sure to taste the compote before you remove it from the heat. If needed, the amount of sugar and lemon juice can be increased or decreased by about 5 percent. This amount of compote will make 12 tartlets. Any extra compote can be frozen.

Select apricots early in the season, when they are just barely ripe, with firm flesh and a pleasant acidity.

The lemon juice is essential in the compote to achieve the desired acidity. The other key to a successful apricot tart is to work quickly, as the fruit changes color rapidly.

Step-by-Step

ASSEMBLING THE APRICOT TARTLETS

01

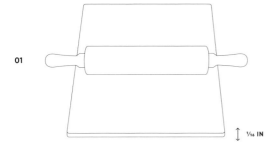

Preheat the oven to 340°F (170°C). Roll the dough to a thickness of about ⅟16 inch (2 mm).

02

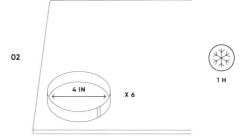

Cut six disks using the pastry cutter. Line the tart rings with the dough: lay the dough over each ring and gently press it into the corners and against the sides. Do not remove any overhanging dough. Place on a baking sheet, and chill in the refrigerator for at least 1 hour to allow the dough to firm up in the ring. Prick the base of the dough all over with a fork.

03

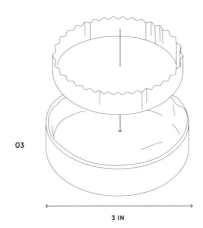

Line each tartlet shell with parchment paper.

04

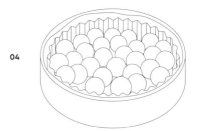

Top with pie weights.

05

25-30 MIN - 340°F (170°C)

Bake for 25 to 30 minutes.

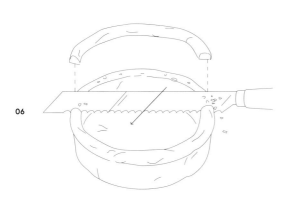

06

Let cool, then use a serrated knife to trim ⅛ inch (2 cm)
off the edges of the tartlet shells.

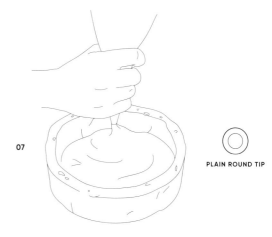

07

PLAIN ROUND TIP

Using a pastry bag fitted with the round tip, pipe pastry cream
to the top of the tartlet shells.

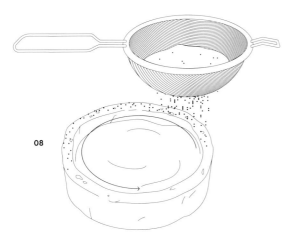

08

Using a fine-mesh sieve, dust the edges with snow sugar.

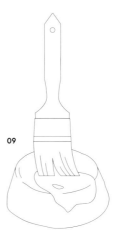

09

Brush the frozen apricot-compote halves with mirror glaze,
and place them on top of the tartlets.

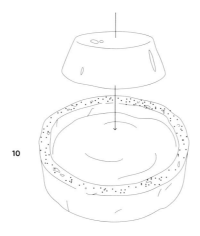

10

Transfer the tartlets to the refrigerator and let thaw
for 1 hour before serving.

Black Sesame Paris-Brest

ACTIVE TIME	RESTING TIME	COOKING TIME
45 minutes	*2 hours*	*35 minutes*

This cake was created for the Japanese embassy in France: they requested a dessert that would showcase a Japanese ingredient. Since I knew that praline paste and sesame work well together, I wanted to use the occasion to combine them in a Paris-Brest.

To be honest, sesame by itself does not have an expansive flavor; it is the praline paste that brings out its qualities. I had heard that French people are not fans of black-colored food. But to my great surprise, this became one of the most popular cakes in the period we offered "Japanese-inspired" pastries in our shop.

Makes 6

EQUIPMENT

1	*pastry bag*
1	*⅔-inch (15-mm) star- or flower-shaped tip*
1	*2 ½-inch (6-cm) tart ring*
1	*2 ½-inch (6-cm) round pastry cutter*
1	*1 ¼-inch (3-cm) round pastry cutter*
1	*silicone baking mat*
1	*stand mixer*

—

BLACK SESAME CRAQUELIN

70 G	*unsalted butter, at room temperature*
40 G	*superfine sugar*
90 G	*all-purpose flour (T55)*
25 G	*black sesame seeds*

—

200 g	*choux pastry* (P. 171)

—

BLACK SESAME LACE

30 G	*unsalted butter*
25 G	*glucose syrup*
50 G	*superfine sugar*
10 G	*chopped blanched almonds*
10 G	*black sesame seeds*
25 G	*pastry flour (T45)*

—

BLACK SESAME PRALINE CREAM

200 G	*pastry cream* (P. 170)
85 G	*unsalted butter, at room temperature*
40 G	*almond praline paste*
40 G	*hazelnut praline paste*
55 G	*black sesame paste*

Black sesame craquelin coating

01.   Stir together the butter, sugar, flour, and sesame seeds in a bowl until well blended and smooth. Let rest in the refrigerator for 2 hours.

Choux pastry

01.   Preheat the oven to 345°F (175°C).

02.   Roll the craquelin coating into a very thin layer (¹⁄₁₆ inch/1 mm) between two sheets of parchment paper. Using the 2 ½-in (6-cm) pastry cutter, cut out six disks, then make a hole in the center of each using the 1 ¼-in (3-cm) pastry cutter.

03.   Grease a baking sheet with butter. Flour the 2 ½-inch (6-cm) ring and use to make six circles on the baking sheet as a template. Fit one of the pastry bags with the star- or flower-shaped tip and fill it with the choux pastry. Pipe out rings of choux pastry around the insides of the circles.

04.   Top each choux ring with a ring of black sesame craquelin, and bake for 25 minutes.

Black sesame lace

01.   Reduce the oven temperature to 320°F (160°C) and line a baking sheet with the silicone baking mat.

02.   In a small saucepan, combine the butter, glucose, and sugar. Bring to a boil, stirring constantly. Place the almonds and black sesame seeds in a large bowl and sift in the flour. Pour in the hot sugar mixture and stir until well combined. Let cool to room temperature.

03.   When the mixture has cooled and hardened, divide it into pieces weighing 3 g each. Place on the prepared baking sheet and bake for 10 minutes, until golden.

Black sesame praline cream

01.   Fit the stand mixer with the whisk attachment and place the pastry cream in the bowl. Beat to loosen, then add the butter, both praline pastes, and the black sesame paste. Beat on low speed until well combined.

Assembly

01.   Using a serrated knife, cut each choux pastry ring in half horizontally. Fit the pastry bag with the star- or flower-shaped tip and fill it with black sesame praline cream. Pipe cream onto the bottom half of each choux ring in a circular pattern, making three layers.

02.   Top each ring with the other half of the choux pastry. To finish, insert pieces of black sesame lace into the cream with the rounded sides facing inward.

—

NOTES: When adding the black sesame paste to the pastry cream, mix until the cream is uniform, with a smooth texture and taste. Do not overbeat the cream, or it may become too light for a Paris-Brest and lose its rich taste, which is what makes the dessert interesting. However, if the cream is not beaten enough, it will collapse. Finding the right balance just takes a little practice.

Tropical Pavlova

ACTIVE TIME	COOKING TIME
45 minutes	*1 hour 40 minutes*

I created this pavlova when I was on the television show Le Meilleur Pâtissier—Les Professionnels. *The theme was "childhood memories." I wanted to create a cake that resembled the fireworks of my youth, which I admired during summer vacations. That experience should come across in the explosion of flavors released with every bite.*

Makes 6

EQUIPMENT

1	*stand mixer*
1	*silicone baking mold with 2 ¾-inch (7-cm) half-spheres*
2	*pastry bags*
1	*¹⁄₁₀-inch (3-mm) plain tip*
1	*⅔-inch (16-mm) star-shaped tip (PF16)*

—

MERINGUES (12 HALF-SPHERES)

12 G	*cornstarch*
125 G	*superfine sugar*
115 G	*egg whites (about 4 whites from large eggs)*
	finely grated zest of ½ yuzu
	neutral oil or cooking spray, for greasing

—

MACERATED FRUIT

60 G	*peeled mango*
35 G	*peeled kiwi*
18 G	*passion fruit pulp and seeds*
	finely grated zest of 1 yuzu
4 G	*yuzu juice*

—

COCONUT WHIPPED CREAM

95 G	*heavy cream, chilled*
8 G	*superfine sugar*
45 G	*coconut purée*

—

DECORATION

coconut oil, melted

Meringues

01.   Preheat the oven to 210°F (100°C).

02.   Combine the cornstarch and sugar in a small bowl. Fit the stand mixer with the whisk attachment, place the egg whites in the bowl and beat until the whites hold medium peaks. Add the cornstarch-sugar mixture in thirds and continue beating until the meringue holds stiff peaks. Turn off the mixer. Using a flexible spatula, fold in the yuzu zest. Transfer the meringue to a pastry bag fitted with the plain tip.

03.   Lightly grease the cavities of the half-sphere mold with neutral oil using a paper towel, or spray with cooking spray. Sprinkle them with sugar to coat, then shake the mold upside down to remove any excess. Place the mold on a baking sheet. Pipe the meringue into the mold: begin at the center, in the bottom of the mold, and pipe in a spiral motion to line the bottom, then the sides, until the entire mold is filled and the meringue forms a hollow half-sphere. Bake for 1 hour and 40 minutes.

04.   Take the meringues out of the oven and turn them out of the mold while they are still hot. When they are cool enough to handle, rub the bottom edges over a fine-mesh sieve to flatten them (so you can form a sphere with two halves).

Macerated fruit

01.   Cut the mango and kiwi into ½-inch (1-cm) cubes. In a bowl, combine them with the pulp and seeds of the passion fruit, and the grated yuzu zest and juice.

Coconut whipped cream

01.   Place the cream, sugar, and coconut purée in the bowl of a stand mixer fitted with the whisk attachment, and beat on high until soft peaks form.

02.   Transfer to a pastry bag fitted with the star-shaped tip.

Assembly and decoration

01.   Pour melted coconut oil into each meringue half-sphere.

02.   Swirl to coat, then pour the oil out and arrange the meringues cut-side up on a baking sheet lined with parchment paper.

03.   Let the meringues rest in the refrigerator for 10 minutes until the coconut oil is firm.

04.   Fill a half-sphere with macerated fruit.

05.   Using the pastry bag fitted with the star-shaped tip, fill another half-sphere with whipped cream.

06.   Put the two halves together to form a sphere, with the whipped cream on the bottom. Repeat until you've formed all 6 spheres.

—

NOTES: It is important to lightly dust the mold with sugar to enhance the meringue's crisp texture.

Coating the inside of the meringue sphere with coconut oil will prevent the meringue from absorbing liquid from the macerated fruit. And because coconut oil melts at body temperature, it will not linger on the palate.

Sicilia

ACTIVE TIME	RESTING TIME	COOKING TIME
1 hour	*9 hours*	*20 minutes*

*I may be a "Japanese pastry chef who makes French pastries," but that doesn't mean that
I can't find inspiration in other culinary cultures, such as American or, in this case, Italian pastry.
This recipe is a nod to the cassata, a Sicilian specialty featuring pistachios.
My creations reflect the inspiration I find on my travels—they are a mix of cultures.*

*But I am not the only one to think this way—I am convinced that no culinary culture
exists in a vacuum. In fact, traditional French pastry bears traces of other cultures, such as Austrian
and Italian traditions in desserts like the Black Forest and Mont Blanc.
Creations travel from country to country, and that is also the beauty of pastry.*

Makes 6

EQUIPMENT

1	*instant-read thermometer*
1	*stand mixer*
2	*stand mixer bowls*
1	*22 x 14 ¼-inch (56 x 36-cm) pastry frame*
1	*1 ¾-inch (7-cm) round pastry cutter*
1	*silicone baking mold with 2 ¾-inch (7-cm) half-spheres*
1	*silicone baking mold with 1 ½-inch (4-cm) half-spheres*
1	*pastry bag*
1	*plain round tip*

—

PISTACHIO JOCONDE SPONGE

280 G	*lightly beaten eggs (about 5½ large eggs), at room temperature*
275 G	*egg whites (about 9 whites from large eggs), at room temperature, divided*
230 G	*almond flour*
145 G	*pistachio flour*
230 G	*confectioners' sugar*
185 G	*unsalted butter*
70 G	*pastry flour (T45)*
85 G	*superfine sugar*

—

MORELLO CHERRY COMPOTE

110 G	*pitted Morello cherries, frozen*
30 G	*superfine sugar*
1 G	*gelatin powder*
5 G	*water, heated to 122°F (50°C)*
3 G	*cornstarch*

→

Pistachio Joconde sponge

01.   Preheat the oven to 340°F (170°C) and place the pastry frame on a baking sheet lined with parchment paper. Whisk together the lightly beaten eggs and 125 g of the egg whites (about 4 whites) in a large bowl set over a saucepan of barely simmering water. Whisking, heat the eggs to about 104°F (40°C). Transfer to one of the stand mixer bowls and fit the mixer with the whisk attachment. Sift together the almond flour, pistachio flour, and confectioners' sugar. Add to the eggs and beat on high speed until the mixture is pale and thick.

02.   Melt the butter to 122°F (50°C) in a large bowl set over a saucepan of barely simmering water. Gradually pour in one-fourth of the beaten egg mixture and whisk continuously until emulsified. Sift the pastry flour into the mixer bowl with the remaining three-fourths of the egg mixture and gently fold it in.

03.   Combine the remaining 150 g egg whites with the superfine sugar in the second mixer bowl and beat with the whisk attachment until the whites hold stiff peaks.

04.   Using a flexible spatula, gently fold the whites into the egg and flour mixture until only a few white streaks remain, then fold in the butter mixture until well blended.

05.   Pour the batter into the pastry frame and smooth it into an even layer using an offset spatula. Bake for 20 minutes, until the cake is set and golden.

06.   Gently slide a spatula between the frame and the sponge to remove the frame. Then, carefully transfer the sponge to a rack and let it cool for 10 minutes.

07.   Once the sponge has cooled completely, cut out 6 disks using the pastry cutter.

Morello cherry compote

01.   Combine the frozen cherries and sugar in a bowl, then let the cherries thaw in the refrigerator. Transfer the cherries and sugar to a saucepan and bring to a boil over medium heat. Remove from the heat and let rest at room temperature for 1 hour. The cherries will release water through osmosis, balancing the sugar at the same time.

02.   In a small bowl, dissolve the gelatin powder in the 122°F (50°C) water. In a separate small bowl, combine one-third of the cherry liquid with the cornstarch. Bring the contents of the saucepan to a boil once again, then add the cornstarch mixture and continue cooking for 2–3 minutes on low heat to release the starch. Stir the dissolved gelatin into the cherry mixture. Transfer the mixture to a bowl, cover with plastic wrap, and place in the refrigerator for about 3 hours, until the gelatin sets.

03.   Place about 12 g cherry compote in the center of each of the 2 ¾-inch (7-cm) half-sphere molds. Let set in the refrigerator.

→

"My pastries are not intended to surprise clients;
that is the role of restaurant desserts.
Above all, I want to delight them with flavor."

MORELLO CHERRY CREAM

1 G	*gelatin powder*
5 G	*water, heated to 122°F (50°C)*
45 G	*superfine sugar*
5 G	*cornstarch*
70 G	*pitted Morello cherries*
7 G	*freshly squeezed lemon juice*
40 G	*lightly beaten egg (about 1 large egg)*
35 G	*egg yolks (about 1 yolk from a large egg)*
40 G	*unsalted butter, at room temperature*
0.2 G	*rose extract*

—

PISTACHIO BAVAROIS

5.3 G	*gelatin powder*
27 G	*water, heated to 122°F (50°C)*
155 G	*whole milk*
45 G	*egg yolks (about 2 yolks from large eggs)*
40 G	*superfine sugar*
40 G	*pistachio paste*
190 G	*heavy cream, whipped to stiff peaks*

—

CHOPPED PISTACHIOS

30	*whole shelled pistachios*
	Fine sea salt

—

DECORATION

	neutral mirror glaze
6	*rose petals*
6	*pistachios, shells on*

Morello cherry cream

01.   In a small bowl, dissolve the gelatin powder in the 122°F (50°C) water. Sift together the sugar and cornstarch. In a small saucepan, bring the cherries and lemon juice to a boil. In a medium bowl, whisk together the eggs and egg yolks with the sugar and cornstarch. Whisking continuously, gradually pour one-third of the warm cherry liquid into the egg mixture. Pour back into the saucepan, whisking continuously. Still whisking, cook over medium heat until the custard thickens and reaches 172°F (78°C). Remove from heat and stir in the butter, then the dissolved gelatin. Combine well.

02.   Transfer the mixture to a bowl and set it over a larger bowl filled with ice water to cool it quickly. When it has cooled, add the rose extract and mix well. Transfer to the pastry bag and pipe 22 g of the mixture into six cavities of the 1 ½-inch (4-cm) half-sphere mold. Place the mold in the freezer for 3 hours, or until frozen.

Pistachio bavarois

01.   In a small bowl, dissolve the gelatin powder in the 122°F (50°C) water. Place the milk in a saucepan and bring to a boil. Combine the egg yolks, sugar, and pistachio paste in a medium bowl and mix well. Whisking continuously, gradually pour one-third of the hot milk into the bowl. Pour back into the saucepan, whisking continuously. Still whisking, cook over medium heat until the custard reaches 172°F (78°C). Remove from heat and stir in the dissolved gelatin. Transfer the mixture to a bowl and set it over a larger bowl filled with ice water until it cools and thickens. Fold in the whipped cream.

02.   Remove the mold containing the cooled cherry compote from the refrigerator. Fill each cavity three-quarters full with bavarois. Nestle the frozen cherry cream half-spheres into the center of the bavarois, then cover with another layer of bavarois. Using a spatula, smooth over the bavarois and remove any excess. Top each with a Joconde sponge disk and place in the freezer for at least 3 hours.

Chopped pistachios

01.   Fill a small saucepan with water and a pinch of salt, and bring to a boil. Add the pistachios and boil for 1 minute. Drain and dry the nuts on a paper towel, then chop them coarsely.

Assembly and decoration

01.   Warm the neutral mirror glaze to 86°F (30°C). Remove the molds from the freezer and turn the gâteaux out of the mold onto a pastry rack. Pour the glaze over each one until it is well-coated.

02.   Press chopped pistachios into the Joconde sponge at the base of each gâteau. Top each with one whole pistachio and 1 rose petal. Let thaw before serving.

NOTES: When it comes to main ingredients for desserts, I believe there should be no more than three elements. In this case, they are Morello cherry, rose, and pistachio—a combination to celebrate spring.

For the cherry compote, be sure to thaw the frozen cherries in the refrigerator. Thawing in hot water or at room temperature brings out an unwelcome acidity.

Crêpe Cake

ACTIVE TIME	RESTING TIME	COOKING TIME
50 minutes	*6 hours*	*50 minutes*

It is interesting that the crêpe, originally from Brittany, traveled to Japan, where it took the form of the mille-crêpe, or crêpe cake, before making its way to other Asian countries. In fact, this cake seems to have been around for four decades already. It is a vagabond with roots in two countries—France and Japan.

The texture of the crème diplomate and the sweet crêpe batter are what make it so irresistible. Of course, it takes a bit of time, but one pan is all you need to prepare this cake. If you are used to making crêpes, this recipe should not be very difficult. Make them the way you usually do!

Serves 10

EQUIPMENT

1	*9 ½-inch (24-cm) crêpe pan or skillet*
1	*stand mixer*

—

CRÊPE BATTER

220 G	*lightly beaten eggs (about 4 ½ large eggs)*
60 G	*superfine sugar*
110 G	*pastry flour (T45)*
35 G	*unsalted butter, melted*
220 G	*whole milk, at room temperature*
	Neutral oil, for cooking

—

WHIPPED CREAM

160 G	*heavy cream, chilled*
16 G	*mascarpone, chilled*
14 G	*superfine sugar*

—

CRÈME DIPLOMATE

635 G	*pastry cream* (P. 170)
190 G	*whipped cream (from above)*

—

DECORATION

snow sugar (non-melting sugar)

Crêpe batter

01.   In a bowl, whisk together the eggs and the sugar. Sift the flour into a large bowl and whisk in a quarter of the egg-sugar mixture. Whisking continuously, gradually pour in the rest of the egg mixture. Whisk in the melted butter. Gradually whisk in the milk. Cover with plastic wrap and let rest in the refrigerator for at least 3 hours.

02.   Warm the pan over medium heat. Place a small amount of neutral oil on a small plate. Lightly dip a piece of paper towel into the oil and wipe it over the pan. Using a ladle, pour just enough batter to create a fine layer in the pan. When the edges begin to brown, turn the crêpe over and let it cook for 10 seconds. Remove to a rack. Repeat until you have 10 crêpes.

Whipped cream

01.   Fit the stand mixer with the whisk attachment and place the cream, mascarpone, and sugar in the bowl. Beat on high speed until stiff peaks form.

Crème diplomate

01.   Place the pastry cream in a bowl and whisk gently to loosen it. Fold in the whipped cream using a flexible spatula.

Assembly and decoration

01.   Spoon 90 g of crème diplomate onto the center of 1 crêpe. Spread it evenly across the surface, starting from the center and working outward, stopping ½ inch (1 cm) from the edge. Top with another crêpe. Repeat with the rest of the crêpes. After you have added the 10th crêpe, let the cake rest in the refrigerator for 3 hours.

02.   Just before serving, cut the cake into 10 equal slices and dust the edges with snow sugar.

Rhubarb Tartlets

ACTIVE TIME	RESTING TIME	COOKING TIME
1 hour	*5 hours*	*30 minutes*

Recently, farmers have begun cultivating rhubarb in northern Japan, but I really began
working with it in France, where it is appreciated for its bright, pleasant acidity.
I wanted to respond to a demand for rhubarb pastries by showcasing the taste of the fruit
without the addition of other flavors.

Makes 12

EQUIPMENT

1	*4 ¼-inch (11-cm) round pastry cutter*
1	*instant-read thermometer*
12	*3 ¼-inch (8-cm) tart rings, ½ inch (1.5 cm) deep*
1	*guitar sheet*
12	*3-inch (7.5-cm) tart rings, ½ inch (1.5-cm) deep pie weights*
1	*pastry bag*
1	*plain round tip*

—

TARTLET SHELLS

480 G	*inverse puff pastry* (P. 172)

—

RHUBARB CREAM

220 G	*red rhubarb*
5 G	*gelatin powder*
25 G	*water, heated to 122°F (50°C)*
130 G	*freshly squeezed lemon juice*
210 G	*superfine sugar, divided*
175 G	*lightly beaten eggs (about 5 ½ large eggs)*
160 G	*egg yolks (about 5 yolks from large eggs)*
21 G	*cornstarch*
175 G	*unsalted butter*

—

RHUBARB COMPOTE

2 G	*gelatin powder*
10 G	*water, heated to 122°F (50°C)*
1.2 KG	*red rhubarb*
340 G	*superfine sugar, divided*
60 G	*freshly squeezed lemon juice*
9 G	*pectin NH*

—

RHUBARB IN SYRUP

1	*stalk red rhubarb*
300 G	*superfine sugar*
300 G	*water*

—

DECORATION

	snow sugar (non-melting sugar)
	neutral mirror glaze

Tartlet shells

01. Roll the puff pastry to a thickness of ¹⁄₁₆ inch (2 mm). Using the 4 ¼-inch (11-cm) pastry cutter, cut out twelve disks of pastry and line each 3 ¼-inch (8-cm) tart ring with the dough: lay the dough over each ring and gently press it into the corners and against the sides. Do not trim the excess dough. Place the shells in the refrigerator for 1 hour.

02. Preheat the oven to 340°F (170°C). Prick the bases of the tartlet shells with a fork. Line the tartlet shells with parchment paper and top with pie weights. Bake for 25 to 30 minutes. Let cool, then use a serrated knife to trim the tartlet edges to ¾ inch (2 cm) high.

Rhubarb cream

01. Wash the rhubarb, then cut it into ¾-inch (2-cm) pieces and place in the freezer for at least 30 minutes, until frozen.

02. In a small bowl, dissolve the gelatin powder in the 122°F (50°C) water. Place the frozen rhubarb, lemon juice, and 100 g of the sugar in a saucepan. Bring to a boil. Place the eggs, egg yolks, remaining 110 g sugar, and cornstarch in a bowl. Mix well. Whisking continuously, gradually pour one-third of the hot rhubarb mixture into the egg mixture, then pour everything back into the saucepan. Stirring nonstop, cook over medium heat until the mixture reaches 172.5°F (78°C). Remove from the heat, add the butter, and mix until smooth. Stir in the dissolved gelatin.

03. Transfer the mixture to a bowl and set it over a larger bowl filled with ice until completely cooled. Press plastic wrap over the surface and reserve in the refrigerator.

Rhubarb compote

01. In a small bowl, dissolve the gelatin powder in the 122°F (50°C) water. Wash the rhubarb, then cut it into ¾-inch (2-cm) pieces and place in the freezer for at least 30 minutes, until frozen.

02. Place the frozen rhubarb pieces, 60 g of the sugar, and the lemon juice in a saucepan and let thaw at room temperature.

03. Once thawed, bring the mixture to a boil, stirring to prevent it from sticking to the bottom of the pan. Reduce the heat to medium and cook for 5 minutes, skimming off any foam that rises to the surface.

04. Combine the pectin and remaining 280 g sugar in a bowl and add them to the saucepan, stirring constantly. Cook over medium heat for 1 minute longer, until the pectin activates and the mixture thickens. Remove from heat and stir in the dissolved gelatin.

05. Line a baking sheet with the guitar sheet and arrange the 3-inch (7.5-cm) tart rings on top. Pour 1 tablespoon of the compote mixture into each ring and place in the freezer for at least 3 hours.

Rhubarb in syrup

01. Preheat the oven to 300°F (150°C). Wash the rhubarb and cut it into 6-inch (15-cm) pieces. Place the sugar and water in a saucepan and bring to a boil, stirring to dissolve the sugar. Place the rhubarb and syrup in a small baking dish. Cut a sheet of parchment paper to fit the dish, then cut a ¾-inch (2 cm) hole in the center of the paper and lay it over the rhubarb.

02. Bake for about 10 minutes, or until the rhubarb is cooked. Let cool to room temperature, then reserve in the refrigerator.

Assembly and decoration

01. Fit the pastry bag with the plain round tip and fill it with the rhubarb cream. Pipe the cream into the tart shells in a spiral. Sprinkle the edges of the puff pastry with snow sugar. Remove the rhubarb compote disks from the freezer. Brush them with a thin layer of mirror glaze and place them over the cream.

02. Remove the rhubarb pieces from the syrup and cut them lengthwise into rectangles, ¹⁄₁₆ inch (2 mm) thick. Then, using one of the 3-inch (7.5-cm) tart rings, cut out half-circles of rhubarb. Arrange these on top of the tartlets.

NOTES: Rhubarb is prepared here in three ways: in a smooth cream, in a compote, and in pieces in a syrup—three variations that contrast with the texture of the puff pastry. When preparing the cream, be sure to leave small pieces of rhubarb, albeit cooked to perfection.

Freezing the rhubarb before cooking helps the stalks release water. Any extra rhubarb compote can be frozen for later use.

Japanese Strawberry Cream Cake

ACTIVE TIME	RESTING TIME	COOKING TIME
1 hour	*1 hour 10 minutes*	*18 minutes*

The fraisier, created a century ago, is the "Japanese cake of French origin" that's the best known and appreciated by Japanese people of all ages. It is eaten at Christmas, for birthdays, on Girls' Day, on Mother's Day, and other special occasions.

It is nearly synonymous with "Western cake." I was not sure whether my French clients were going to like it; French people tend to prefer foods that have body, unlike the Japanese, who love anything with a foamy, melty texture. Nevertheless, my version of this cake quickly gained a following; today, French people are fond of different textures. I enjoy sharing with them some of the flavors that have shaped me, and I am overjoyed when a client compliments me on my fraisier.

Serves 4 to 5

EQUIPMENT

1	*stand mixer*
2	*stand mixer bowls*
1	*instant-read thermometer*
1	*21 ¼ × 13 ¾-inch (54 × 35-cm) pastry frame*
1	*6-inch (15-cm) round pastry cutter*
1	*pastry bag*
1	*¾-inch (2-cm) petal tip*

—

"SOUFFLÉ" SPONGE

160 G	*whole milk*
90 G	*unsalted butter*
125 G	*pastry flour (T45)*
6 G	*baking powder*
400 G	*egg whites (about 13 whites from large eggs), divided*
190 G	*egg yolks (about 9 yolks from large eggs)*
180 G	*superfine sugar*
3.5 G	*egg white powder*

STRAWBERRY SIMPLE SYRUP

40 G	*superfine sugar*
85 G	*water*
25 G	*strawberry purée*

—

WHIPPED CREAM

650 G	*heavy cream*
65 G	*mascarpone, chilled*
60 G	*superfine sugar*

—

ASSEMBLY

200 G	*strawberries, preferably Gariguette*

—

DECORATION

	whole strawberries, preferably Gariguette

"Soufflé" sponge

01.   Preheat the oven to 340°F (170°C) and place the pastry frame on a baking sheet lined with parchment paper. Combine the milk and butter in a small saucepan and bring to a boil. Fit the stand mixer with the whisk attachment and sift the flour and baking powder together into the bowl, then add the hot milk mixture and beat on medium speed until well blended.

02.   Whisk together the egg yolks and 80 g of the egg whites (about 2½ whites) in a bowl set over a saucepan of barely simmering water. Whisking, heat the egg mixture to about 86°F (30°C), then pour it into the mixer bowl with the milk and flour mixture and beat until smooth.

03.   To prepare a meringue, whisk together the sugar and egg white powder in a bowl until well blended. Place the remaining 325 g egg whites (about 10 whites) in the second mixer bowl and beat until the whites hold medium peaks, then add the sugar mixture and beat until the meringue holds firm peaks. Immediately fold the meringue into the rest of the batter just until no white streaks remain.

04.   Pour the batter into the pastry frame on the baking sheet and smooth it into an even layer using an offset spatula. Bake for 18 minutes, or until the surface is golden and springs back when lightly touched.

05.   Gently slide a spatula between the frame and the sponge to remove the frame and transfer the sponge to a rack. Let it cool for 10 minutes, then press plastic wrap into the golden surface and let the sponge rest at room temperature for at least 1 hour.

06.   Gently peel off the plastic wrap to remove the sponge's browned surface. Remove the parchment paper. Use the pastry cutter to cut out three disks of sponge.

Strawberry simple syrup

01.   Place the sugar and water in a saucepan and bring to a boil, stirring to dissolve the sugar, then let the mixture cool. Add the strawberry purée and mix well.

Whipped cream

01.   Fit the stand mixer with the whisk attachment and place the cream, mascarpone, and sugar in the bowl. Beat on high speed almost until medium peaks form. Reserve half the cream, then continue to beat the remaining cream on high speed until stiff peaks form.

NOTES: Except for the strawberries, Japanese strawberry cream cakes have nothing in common with their French counterparts. I wanted to make my own version to satisfy the French palate. Aware of the difference in texture between French and Japanese versions of the cake layer, I came up with my own by adding meringue to a choux pastry.

Also, just as in the Japanese version, I do not add vanilla to the cream. This makes it easier to fully appreciate the flavor of the strawberries.

Assembly and decoration

SEE THE STEP-BY-STEP INSTRUCTIONS ON PAGES 62–63.

→

Step-by-Step

ASSEMBLING
THE JAPANESE STRAWBERRY CREAM CAKE

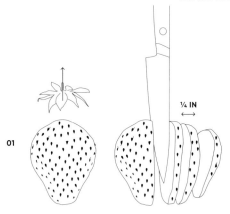

01 Hull the strawberries and cut into ¼-inch (7-mm) slices.

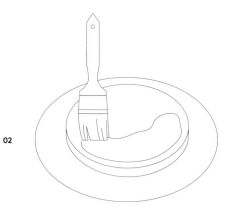

02 Place a disk of sponge on a plate. Brush the surface with the strawberry simple syrup.

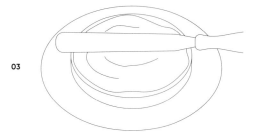

03 Spread a ½-inch (1-cm) layer of the cream whipped to medium peaks over the surface of the sponge using a spatula.

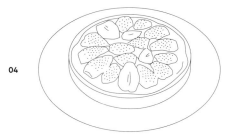

04 Arrange about fifteen strawberry pieces over the cream.

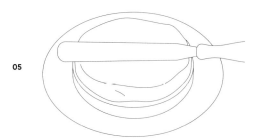

05 Spread another layer of the medium-peak whipped cream over the strawberries, making sure the pieces are covered.

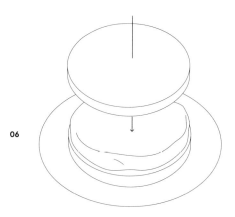

06 Top with another disk of cake. Repeat the previous 4 steps and finish with the third disk of cake.

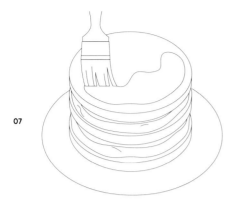

07

Soak the top of the last disk with the strawberry syrup.

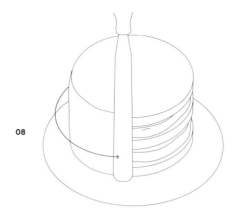

08

Using a spatula, smooth and cover all sides of the cake with the cream whipped to stiff peaks.

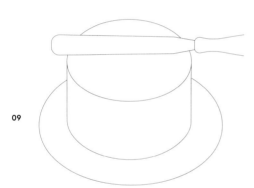

09

Spread a layer of the cream whipped to medium peaks over the top and sides of the cake to a thickness of about ½ inch (1 cm).

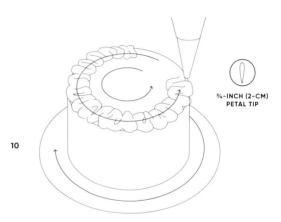

¾-INCH (2-CM) PETAL TIP

10

Fit the pastry bag with the petal tip and fill it with cream whipped to medium peaks and pipe petals all around the cake.

11

Finish by placing whole strawberries on top of the cake.

25 Avenue de Breteuil, Paris 7th Arrondissement – 12:20 pm

CHAP. 3

Noon

Saint-Tropez Tart

ACTIVE TIME	RESTING TIME	COOKING TIME
45 minutes	*6 hours*	*20 minutes*

I must admit that when I tried a Saint-Tropez tart for the first time, I was not particularly impressed.
I tasted it in order to learn more about French pastry and to find inspiration, but the cake's orange blossom flavor
and heavy appearance put me off. I had to try it two or three more times before I could appreciate it.
This is a cake to be savored in a relaxed atmosphere.

Today, many of my customers eat it across the street from my shop, settled comfortably in the grass.
And I am delighted that they can eat it surrounded by friends and family. This Saint-Tropez Tart has become
a classic. I think it may even be the best recipe for showcasing brioche.

Serves 8

EQUIPMENT

1	*7 ¾-inch (20-cm) tart ring, ¾ inch (2 cm) deep*
1	*stand mixer*
1	*pastry bag*
1	*½-inch (12-mm) plain tip*

—

BRIOCHE

250 G	*brioche dough* (BRIOCHE NANTERRE, P. 22)
50 G	*pearl sugar*
	unsalted butter, for greasing

—

EGG WASH

50 G	*egg yolks (about 2 yolks from large eggs)*
5 G	*heavy cream*

—

ORANGE BLOSSOM SYRUP

35 G	*water*
19 G	*sugar*
2 G	*orange blossom water*

—

WHIPPED CREAM

70 G	*heavy cream, chilled*
7 G	*mascarpone, chilled*
6 G	*superfine sugar*
4 G	*orange blossom water*

—

CRÈME DIPLOMATE

265 G	*pastry cream* (P. 170)
80 G	*heavy cream, whipped to stiff peaks*

—

DECORATION

	snow sugar (non-melting sugar)

Brioche

01.   Prepare brioche dough. After the second rise, remove 250 g of dough and form a ball. Roll the dough into a disk 7 to 7 ½ inches (18 to 19 cm) wide and ¼ inch (8 mm) thick. Grease the inside of the tart ring with butter, then line it with a strip of parchment paper 1 ¼ inch (3 cm) wide, so that it extends past the ring by ½ inch (1 cm). Line a baking sheet with parchment paper and place the ring on top.

02.   Place the brioche dough inside the tart ring and prick all over with a fork. Place in an unheated oven with a bowl of warm water (approximately 86°F/30°C) inside to keep the air moist and encourage the dough to rise. Let rise for 2 ½ to 3 hours, until approximately doubled in size.

03.   Preheat the oven to 340°F (170°C). Prepare the egg wash: in a bowl, whisk together the egg yolks and cream. Brush over the dough and sprinkle the surface with pearl sugar. Bake for 20 minutes. Remove the ring and transfer the brioche to a rack to cool.

Orange blossom syrup

01.   Place the water and sugar in a saucepan. Bring to a boil, stirring to dissolve the sugar, then let cool and stir in the orange blossom water.

Whipped cream

01.   Fit the stand mixer with the whisk attachment and place the cream, mascarpone, sugar, and orange blossom water in the bowl. Beat on high speed until stiff peaks form.

Crème diplomate

01.   Place the pastry cream in a bowl and gently whisk to loosen it. Fold in the whipped cream using a flexible spatula. Avoid overmixing, or the cream will be too soft. Transfer to a pastry bag fitted with the plain tip.

Assembly and decoration

01.   Cut the brioche in half horizontally. Soak each exposed half of the brioche with about 50 g of the orange blossom syrup. Pipe the crème diplomate onto the bottom half of the cut brioche in a spiral. Top with the other half of the brioche and sprinkle with snow sugar. Place in the refrigerator for 30 minutes, until the cream sets and the brioche has soaked up the syrup.

NOTES: To ensure a moist brioche, be generous when brushing on the syrup.

Black Currant Polonaise

ACTIVE TIME	RESTING TIME	COOKING TIME
1 hour	*12 hours + 1 hour*	*15 minutes*

Have you ever tasted a Polonaise? This traditional cake is in danger of extinction, most likely because it is so complex to make. But there is no reason that anyone who likes rum baba shouldn't appreciate this dessert. In fact, I suspect that the baba and the Polonaise both came about as clever ways of using day-old brioche.

In the classic version, the brioche is soaked in a syrup made with alcohol, and candied orange peel is added to the crème diplomate. Candied cherries are added for decoration. But I decided to modernize this cake.

Makes 6

EQUIPMENT

1	*2-inch (5-cm) round pastry cutter*
1	*instant-read thermometer*
1	*refractometer (optional)*
1	*stand mixer*
2	*pastry bags*
1	*½-inch (12-mm) plain tip*
1	*8-tooth log (bûche) tip cake turntable*

—

BRIOCHE

2	*Brioche Nanterre loaves (P. 22)*
	confectioners' sugar

—

BLACK CURRANT SYRUP

195 G	*water*
95 G	*sugar*
10 G	*black currant purée*

—

BLACK CURRANT JAM

115 G	*black currant purée*
85 G	*superfine sugar, divided*
2 G	*pectin NH*

→

Dehydrated fresh black currants

01.   The day before baking, freeze 42 fresh black currants until frozen solid. Remove them from the freezer and let them drain on parchment paper, at room temperature, overnight.

Brioche

01.   Freeze the brioche loaves. Preheat the oven to 340°F (170°C). Cut the frozen loaves into 1-inch (2.5-cm) slices, then using the pastry cutter, cut twelve 2-inch (5-cm) disks out of the slices. Place the disks on a baking rack, dust them with confectioners' sugar, and bake for 7 minutes, until golden brown.

Black currant syrup

01.   Combine the water, sugar, and black currant purée in a saucepan. Bring to a boil, stirring, then let cool to about 122°F (50°C). Soak the baked brioche disks in the syrup for about 30 seconds, then place them on a rack to drain. Let the brioche cool in the refrigerator.

Black currant jam

01.   Place the black currant purée and 75 g of sugar in a saucepan over medium heat. If you have a refractometer, use it to check the sugar content. Continue to cook until the mixture reaches 56° Brix. If you don't have a refractometer, let the mixture cook at a boil for 5 minutes. Stir in the pectin and remaining 10 g of sugar. Stirring continuously, cook for 30 more seconds to activate the pectin, allowing it to set. Transfer to a bowl, press plastic wrap over the surface, and reserve in the refrigerator.

→

> **"I want to create cakes that don't 'lie,'
> that aren't disguised. Like someone sincere,
> someone you can trust."**

CRÈME DIPLOMATE AND
FROZEN BRIOCHE COMPONENTS

2 G	*gelatin powder*
10 G	*water heated to 122°F (50°C)*
165 G	*pastry cream* (P. 170)
2 G	*crème de cassis (black currant liqueur)*
40 G	*heavy cream, whipped to stiff peaks*
30	*fresh black currants*

—

BLACK CURRANT ITALIAN
MERINGUE

100 G	*egg whites (about 3 whites from large eggs)*
205 G	*superfine sugar*
35 G	*glucose syrup*
65 G	*water*
55 G	*black currant jam*

—

DECORATION

	toasted sliced almonds
42	*dehydrated fresh black currants (from above)*
	confectioners' sugar

Crème diplomate and frozen brioche components

01.   In a small bowl, dissolve the gelatin powder in the 122°F (50°C) water. Place the pastry cream in a large bowl and gently whisk to loosen it. Place one-third of the pastry cream in a separate bowl and stir in the dissolved gelatin until well combined, then fold this mixture into the remaining pastry cream. In a third bowl, whisk together the crème de cassis and whipped cream, then fold this mixture into the pastry cream.

02.   Transfer the crème diplomate to a pastry bag fitted with the ½-inch (12-mm) tip and pipe 20 g onto the center of 6 of the brioche disks. Arrange three fresh black currants on the cream, then pipe 5 g of black currant jam into the center of each.

03.   Top each with another brioche disk. Pipe 10 g of crème diplomate onto the center of each and arrange two fresh currants on the cream. Place in the freezer for 1 hour.

Black currant Italian meringue

01.   Place the egg whites in the bowl of the stand mixer fitted with the whisk attachment and beat on medium speed to soft peaks. Meanwhile, place the sugar, glucose, and water in a saucepan and heat to 239°F (115°C).

02.   Whisking continuously, slowly pour the syrup in a thin stream down the side of the bowl, and beat until the meringue holds stiff peaks. Incorporate the black currant jam. Using a flexible spatula, transfer the meringue to a pastry bag fitted with the bûche tip.

Assembly and baking

SEE THE STEP-BY-STEP INSTRUCTIONS ON PAGE 71.

NOTES: I replaced the candied orange peel with black currant because of its acidity, which gives this classic, sweet cake, a certain balance.

Step-by-Step

ASSEMBLING THE BLACK CURRANT POLONAISE

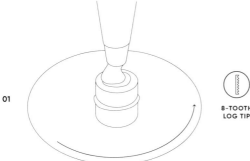

01

8-TOOTH LOG TIP

02

Preheat the oven to 390°F (200°C). Remove the frozen brioche components from the freezer and place them one at a time on a cake turntable. Working from top to bottom, pipe the Italian meringue onto the frozen component, rotating the cake turntable with your other hand. The brioche should be completely covered in meringue when you finish.

Using a cake spatula and working from top to bottom, gently press into the top of the polonaise, flattening and rotating the cake turntable, as you move the spatula evenly down the meringue. This will create an even spiral around the whole cake.

03

04

Working from top to bottom and around the dome, press the sliced almonds onto the meringue.

Do the same with seven dehydrated black currants. Repeat with the remaining frozen components.

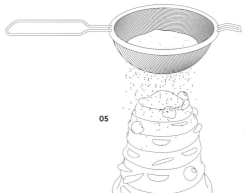

05

MIN AT 390°F (200°C)

Dust each Polonaise with confectioners' sugar. Bake for about 5 minutes, until the meringue is dry and just beginning to color.

Hazelnut Millefeuille

ACTIVE TIME	RESTING TIME	COOKING TIME
45 minutes	*1 hour*	*45 minutes*

Hazelnuts have always been one of my favorite ingredients.
I love their intense flavor, and when I arrived in France, I sought out richly-flavored varieties
of hazelnut pastries. Encouraged by this discovery, I decided to create a millefeuille using a cream similar
to the one in a Paris-Brest: as dense as it is rich, and balanced by the lightness of the inverse puff pastry.

I chose hazelnut praline because it adds a bit of crunch and complements the already crisp puff pastry.

Makes 8 servings

EQUIPMENT

1	*stand mixer*
2	*pastry bags*
1	*½-inch (11-mm) plain tip*

—

INVERSE PUFF PASTRY

| 860 G | *inverse puff pastry* (P. 172) |
| 80 G | *glucose syrup* |

HAZELNUT CREAM

560 G	*pastry cream* (P. 170)
480 G	*hazelnut praline paste*
320 G	*unsalted butter, at room temperature*

—

DECORATION

| 18 | *nougatine hazelnuts* (SEE CHOCOLATE TART, P. 132), *halved hazelnut praline paste* |

Inverse puff pastry

01.   Roll the puff pastry to a thickness of ⅟₁₆ inch (2 mm). Prick the dough all over with a fork. Cut out a 20 ½ × 13 ½-inch (52 × 34-cm) rectangle. Transfer the pastry to a baking sheet lined with parchment paper and let rest in the refrigerator for 1 hour.

02.   Preheat the oven to 340°F (170°C). Bake the pastry for 12 minutes, or until it rises. Remove from the oven and cover the pastry with parchment paper. Top with a baking sheet and press down. Return to the oven for a further 10 minutes. Rotate the baking sheet 180° and bake for a further 5 to 10 minutes.

03.   Meanwhile, heat the glucose in the microwave for 30 seconds. Remove the pastry from the oven and brush the surface with a thin layer of glucose. Return the pastry to the oven for a further 5 minutes, until the glucose dries. Remove the pastry from the oven again. Turn it over and brush the other side with a thin layer of glucose. Return to the oven for a further 5 minutes, until the glucose dries. Remove from the oven and let the pastry cool completely. Cut the pastry into three 8 ½ × 6 ¼-inch (22 × 16-cm) rectangles.

Hazelnut cream

01.   Fit the stand mixer fitted with the whisk attachment and place the pastry cream, hazelnut praline paste, and butter in the bowl. Beat on high speed, but stop before the mixture becomes pale and thick, otherwise the cream will have a too-light mouthfeel and lose its thick texture. Transfer to a pastry bag fitted with the ½-inch (11-mm) tip.

Assembly and decoration

01.   Pipe 7 rows of 10 mounds of hazelnut cream onto a sheet of puff pastry. Top with another sheet of puff pastry and pipe another set of cream mounds. Repeat with the last sheet of puff pastry.

02.   Using the other pastry bag (without a tip), pipe hazelnut praline paste between the pearls of cream. Finally, top every other cream mound with a nougatine hazelnut half.

NOTES: Pressing the puff pastry during baking results in uniform layers, and using glucose rather than sugar achieves a crunchier texture.

Mystery Baba

ACTIVE TIME	RESTING TIME	COOKING TIME
1 hour	*1 hour*	*20 to 25 minutes*

When I first opened my shop, I made a classic rum baba, although I hadn't found the "best answer" to this cake. But at some point, to give it a more contemporary aspect, I sought out ingredients to replace the alcohol that would be as heady as the rum. Enter passion fruit.

Then I approached the baba dough as an ingredient, and I developed a delicious cake served in the skin of the passion fruit. I wanted the end result to look like a mysterious fruit.

Makes 6

EQUIPMENT

1	*instant-read thermometer*
1	*stand mixer*
2	*pastry bags*
1	*silicone baking mold with 2 ¼-inch (7-cm) half-spheres*
1	*½-inch (12-mm) plain tip*

—

BABA DOUGH

6 G	*fresh yeast*
75 G	*whole milk*
40 G	*unsalted butter, divided*
150 G	*all-purpose flour (T55)*
3 G	*fine sea salt*
12 G	*granulated sugar*
80 G	*lightly beaten eggs (about 2 large eggs), cold*

—

PASSION FRUIT SYRUP

500 G	*water*
225 G	*superfine sugar*
100 G	*passion fruit purée*
25 G	*mango purée*
50 G	*freshly squeezed lemon juice*

—

PASSION FRUIT PASTRY CREAM

210 G	*pastry cream (P. 170), cooled*
21 G	*passion fruit purée*
40 G	*mango purée*

—

PASSION FRUIT GLAZE

130 G	*neutral mirror glaze*
21 G	*passion fruit purée*
50 G	*mango purée*

—

ASSEMBLY AND DECORATION

3	*fresh passion fruits unsweetened desiccated coconut*

Baba dough

01.   Dissolve the yeast in the milk. Melt 10 g of the butter, then let cool to 86°F (30 °C). Fit the stand mixer with the dough hook and place the flour, salt, sugar, and cooled melted butter in the bowl. Add the yeast mixture. Begin kneading on medium speed for 5 minutes. Increase to high speed and gradually add the eggs.

02.   When the eggs have been incorporated and the dough begins to pull away from the sides, check to see if the gluten is well developed and passes the "windowpane" test: gently stretch a little dough. If it stretches until thin and translucent without tearing, it's ready; if not, keep kneading.

03.   Add the remaining 30 g butter at high speed until well incorporated. Gather the dough into a ball and transfer it to a bowl. Cover with plastic wrap and let rest, at room temperature, for 20 minutes (first rise).

04.   Use a flexible spatula to remove any air bubbles and ensure the dough is well blended, then transfer it to a pastry bag fitted with the round tip. Pipe approximately 24 g of dough into six cavities of the half-sphere mold. Let rest for 40 minutes at room temperature 78°F (26°C) (second rise).

05.   Preheat the oven to 320°F (160°C). Bake the babas for 20 to 25 minutes, then turn them out onto a rack and let them cool completely.

Passion fruit syrup

01.   Place the water, sugar, passion fruit and mango purées, and lemon juice in a saucepan and heat to 176°F (80°C), stirring until the sugar dissolves completely. Let cool to 113° to 122°F (45° to 50°C).

02.   Soak the babas in the syrup, round side down, for 10 minutes. Then turn them over and let the syrup soak through to the center for about 5 minutes. Remove the babas from the syrup and return them to the rack. Place in the refrigerator to cool.

Passion fruit pastry cream

01.   Place the pastry cream in a bowl and stir in the passion fruit and mango purées until smooth. Transfer to a pastry bag.

Passion fruit glaze

01.   Combine the mirror glaze and passion fruit and mango purées in a bowl and heat to 86°F (30°C). Take the babas out of the refrigerator and immediately pour the hot glaze over them.

Assembly and decoration

01.   Halve each passion fruit and scoop the pulp into a bowl. Clean the passion fruit shells well.

02.   Using a sharp knife, trim the base of each shell flat so they will be stable. Place a few passion fruit seeds on the inside of each shell, then fill with passion fruit pastry cream.

03.   Place a baba on top of each shell and sprinkle a few passion fruit seeds on top. Finally, press desiccated coconut onto the sides of the babas.

NOTES: The passion fruit and mango make the dough especially moist. Ultimately, the result is a dessert quite different from the traditional rum baba, but one that nevertheless brings out the potential of the baba pastry. It goes without saying that you should choose ripe passion fruit and mangoes when they are in season.

When making baba dough, it is essential to pay close attention to temperature and cooking time. This is no easy task, even for a professional pastry chef. So don't be discouraged if the result isn't perfect the first time.

Also, try not to overcook the babas, so that the color of the passion fruit glaze will stand out.

Banana Crème Brûlée

ACTIVE TIME
45 minutes

COOKING TIME
35 minutes

When I was a child, I loved the banana shakes served at the tearoom my parents used to take me to. Bananas were a luxury back then…. I wish there were more banana cakes in France, because bananas go so well with dairy products and eggs. The banana crème brûlée was one of my first professional creations. This is probably why I am particularly fond of this recipe.

I developed it in 2003, when I was twenty-five and working in a hotel in Japan. I had to come up with a dessert for lunch. I wanted to make a nourishing and energizing dessert that wouldn't be sickly-sweet in hot weather. Since everyone loves bananas, I made several attempts with the fruit and discovered their harmonious pairing with dairy, and that their creamy texture approximates that of crème brûlée. Finally, I discovered that putting caramelized banana at the bottom of the ramekin before adding the cream brought out the taste of the fruit even more.

Makes 5

EQUIPMENT

5	*crème brûlée ramekins*
1	*pastry bag*
1	*kitchen blowtorch*

—

BANANA COMPOTE

20 G	*superfine sugar*
15 G	*unsalted butter*
210 G	*ripe banana, peeled and cut into 1 ¼-inch (3-cm) pieces*
15 G	*freshly squeezed lemon juice*

—

CRÈME BRÛLÉE

200 G	*whole milk*
200 G	*heavy cream*
⅓	*vanilla bean, split lengthwise*
75 G	*egg yolks (about 3 yolks from large eggs)*
60 G	*demerara sugar*
60 G	*peeled ripe banana*

—

DECORATION

demerara sugar

Banana compote

01.   In a small heavy saucepan, heat the sugar until it melts and caramelizes. Gently swirl the pan. As soon as fine bubbles appear on the surface, remove the pan from the heat and add the butter to stop the cooking. Stir until smooth.

02.   Add the banana pieces, mashing them with a whisk. Add the lemon juice and cook over medium heat for 2 minutes, stirring continuously. Transfer the compote to a bowl, cover with plastic wrap, and reserve in the refrigerator.

03.   When the compote has cooled, transfer it to a pastry bag and pipe 50 g into each ramekin.

Crème brûlée

01.   Combine the milk and cream in a large saucepans. With the tip of a paring knife, scrape in the vanilla seeds. Bring to a boil, then remove from the heat.

02.   Meanwhile, in a bowl, whisk together the egg yolks and sugar until well blended. Whisking continuously, gradually pour the egg mixture into the saucepan with the milk and cream.

03.   Place the banana in a bowl and mash it using a flexible spatula until it is smooth and almost liquid, then add it to the saucepan. Stir until well combined. Divide the mixture between the ramekins.

04.   Preheat the oven to 310°F (155°C). Place the ramekins in a deep baking dish and pour in enough water to come just past halfway up the sides of the ramekins. Bake for 35 minutes, until the custard remains set when the ramekins are gently shaken. Remove the ramekins from the water bath and let the custard cool to room temperature, then transfer the ramekins to the refrigerator.

Decoration

01.   Sprinkle each crème brûlée with a thin layer of demerara sugar and melt with the blowtorch.

02.   Sprinkle more demerara sugar over the entire surface, and melt again with the torch to obtain a golden crust of caramelized sugar.

NOTES: The banana adds extra creaminess to the crème brûlée. Make sure to chill the dessert; it is too soft when warm.

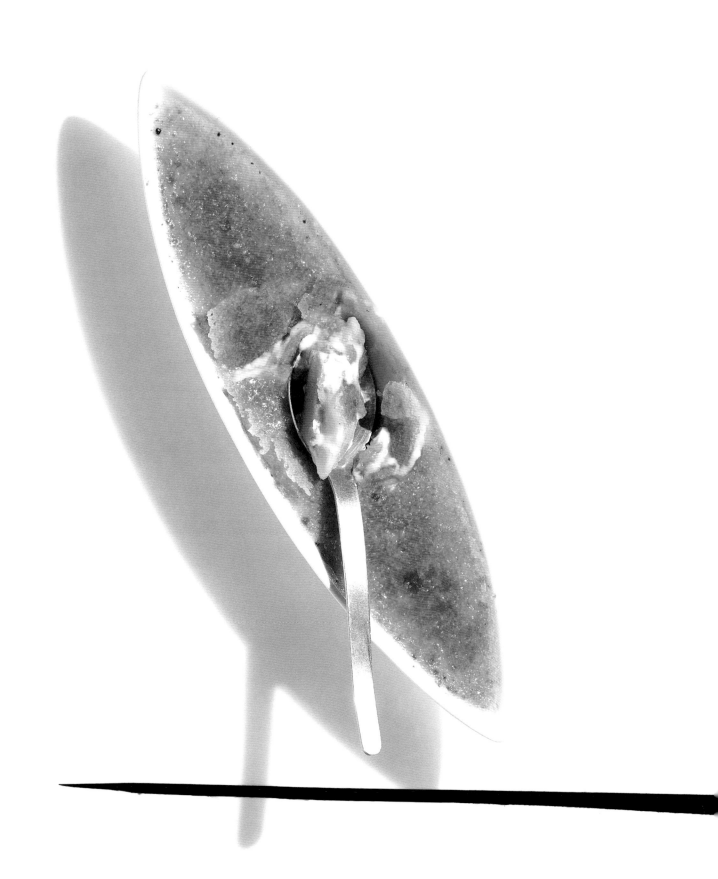

Lemon King Cake

ACTIVE TIME	**RESTING TIME**	**COOKING TIME**
30 minutes	*30 minutes*	*45 minutes*

Each year around Epiphany (January 6), we make many galettes, or king cakes, in our store. I enjoy seeing that our clients relish them, because I consider elements like almond cream and pastry cream to be foundational components of traditional pâtisserie.

When I arrived in Paris, I didn't see much interest in this very simple cake; much like the Saint-Tropez Tart, the steps are basic, and it contains few ingredients. But over time, and after living in France, I came to understand why people get excited about this festive cake, and I decided I wanted to revisit the basics to create my own version.

Serves 4

EQUIPMENT

1	*pastry bag*
1	*½-inch (12-mm) plain tip*
1	*7 ¾-inch (20-cm) tart ring cake turntable*

—

SEMI-CONFIT LEMON PEEL

580 G	*water, divided*
60 G	*lemon peel, cut into ¼-inch (5 to 6 mm) pieces*
80 G	*sugar*
40 G	*freshly squeezed lemon juice (from 1 or 2 lemons, depending on their size)*

—

LEMON FRANGIPANE

165 G	*almond cream* (P. 177)
70 G	*pastry cream* (P. 170)
	finely grated zest of ½ lemon
15 G	*semi-confit lemon peel* (SEE ABOVE)
1	*dried fava bean*

—

ASSEMBLY

400 G	*inverse puff pastry* (P. 172)
	egg white

—

EGG WASH

50 G	*egg yolks (about 2 ½ yolks from large eggs)*
3 G	*heavy cream*

Galette

01.   Roll the puff pastry to a thickness of -inch (2-mm) and cut it into two 9 ½-inch (24-cm) squares. And then renumber the text below

Semi-confit lemon peel

01.   In a saucepan, bring 500 g of the water to a boil, then add the lemon peel. Cook over high heat for 1 minute to remove the bitterness, then drain the peels.

02.   In another saucepan, bring the sugar, lemon juice, and the remaining 80 g water to a boil. Add the drained lemon peel and cook over medium heat for 5 minutes. Transfer the peel to a bowl, cover with plastic wrap, and let cool in the refrigerator.

Lemon frangipane

01.   Place the almond cream in a bowl. Whisk the pastry cream to loosen it, then fold it into the almond cream using a flexible spatula. Stir in the lemon zest and 15 g of the semi-confit lemon peel.

02.   Line a baking sheet with parchment paper. Transfer the frangipane to the pastry bag fitted with the ½-inch (12-mm) tip and pipe a spiral 6 ¼ inches (16 cm) in diameter onto the parchment paper. Hide the fava bean in the frangipane and chill in the refrigerator for 15 minutes.

Assembly and baking

01.   Using a spatula, slide the lemon frangipane onto the center of one of the puff pastry squares. Brush a thin layer of egg white around the edges. Place the second puff pastry square on top, turning it 45°. Be careful not to let any air enter between the frangipane and the pastry. Seal the two layers of pastry by pressing firmly on the edges. Place the galette in the refrigerator for 15 minutes.

02.   Place the 7 ¾-inch (20-cm) tart ring over the galette and press down to trim the edges and create a circle. To prepare the egg wash, whisk together the egg yolks and cream. Brush over the entire surface of the galette and refrigerate until the wash is halfway dry. Repeat with another layer of egg wash and return to the refrigerator until the wash is completely dry.

03.   Preheat the oven to 340°F (170°C). Place the galette on the cake turntable. Make a ¼-inch (5-mm) hole in the center. Place the tip of a knife in the center of the galette, beside the hole, and, rotating the cake turntable, trace a spiral groove across the entire surface of the galette (don't cut all the way through the pastry). Then make 5 equally-spaced incisions around the circumference of the galette in the groove, cutting through the pastry, to let steam escape. Cut incisions along the outer edge of the galette to create a scalloped border.

04.   Insert a small tube of parchment paper into the hole at the center of the galette to form a chimney that will allow steam to escape during baking. Bake for 45 minutes.

NOTES: This version of king cake combines my two great loves—a classic cake and citrus fruit.

The base is still frangipane; it just has a touch more lemon.

MORI YOSHIDA
Paris

Golden Tarte Tatin

ACTIVE TIME	COOKING TIME
1 hour	*2 hours 25 minutes*

To be honest, I don't put much stock in the legends surrounding certain recipes, like the one that claims the Tarte Tatin was the result of an accident—a culinary misstep. A cake is nothing other than the result of a chef's unending reflection and innumerable experimentations.

What would the Tatin sisters create if they were alive today and had access to the techniques and tools we are so familiar with? This is my response to that question.

Serves 6

EQUIPMENT

1	*7 ¾-inch (20-cm) round cake pan, 2 ¾ inches (7 cm) deep*
1	*sous vide bag*
1	*sous vide cooker (optional)*
1	*stand mixer*

—

TATIN

190 G	*inverse puff pastry* (P. 172)
2.2 G	*Golden Delicious apples (1.5 kg when peeled and cored)*
600 G	*superfine sugar, divided*
7 G	*pectin NH*
27 G	*freshly squeezed lemon juice*

—

WHIPPED CREAM

100 G	*heavy cream, cold*
10 G	*mascarpone, cold*
9 G	*superfine sugar*
¼	*vanilla bean, split lengthwise*

—

DECORATION

	neutral mirror glaze
	ground cinnamon

Tarte Tatin

01.   Preheat the oven to 340°F (170°C) and line a baking sheet with parchment paper. Roll the puff pastry to a thickness of 1/16 inch (2 mm) and shape it into a 9 ½-inch (24-cm) square. Place on the prepared baking sheet and bake for 30 minutes. Using the cake pan as a guide, cut out a 7 ¾-inch (20-cm) disk of puff pastry.

02.   Peel and core the apples, then cut each into eight equal slices. Combine 450 g of the sugar and the pectin in a large bowl. Stir in the lemon juice, then add the sliced apples and toss to combine. Transfer this mixture to a sous vide bag and seal. Immerse the bag in boiling water, lower the heat, and simmer over low heat for 20 to 30 minutes.

03.   Preheat the oven to 340°F (170°C). Remove the apples from the bag and drain the syrup into a saucepan. Gently toss the apples with the remaining sugar and arrange them in the cake pan.

04.   Place the saucepan with the syrup over medium heat and reduce the syrup by 60 percent. Pour 250 g of the syrup over the apples in the pan.

05.   Bake for 45 minutes.

06.   Place the ring of puff pastry on top of the apples and bake for an additional 30 to 40 minutes. Lift the puff pastry to see if the apples are deeply golden. If not, let the tart bake for a few more minutes. Cool at room temperature.

Whipped cream

01.   Fit the stand mixer with the whisk attachment and place the cream, mascarpone, and sugar in the bowl. With the tip of a paring knife, scrape in the vanilla seeds.

02.   Beat on high speed until stiff peaks form.

Decoration

01.   Warm the pan slightly over a flame to make turning out the tart easier. Invert a plate on top of the tart, and, holding the pan and the plate firmly together, flip everything upside down. Carefully remove the pan. Brush a thin layer of mirror glaze over the top of the tart.

02.   Cut the tart into equal pieces. Place 1 teaspoon of whipped cream on each slice and sprinkle with a pinch of cinnamon.

NOTES: When cooking sous vide, turning down the heat after adding the apples prevents them from breaking. Through osmosis, the water released from the apples will combine with the sugar to produce a syrup.

2 Place du Palais Royal, Paris 1st Arrondissement – 2:15 p.m.

CHAP. 4

2 p.m.

2 P.M.

Cheesecake

ACTIVE TIME	RESTING TIME	COOKING TIME
1 hour	*1 hour + 12 hours*	*18 minutes*
		+ 2 hours 30 minutes

*It took me three years to develop a cheesecake that would be well-received by the French.
When I first arrived in France, I had a hard time figuring out a place for this dessert after the cheese
plate. After some experimentation, I ended up with this improved version of a New York-style
cheesecake I'd learned to make while working at an American hotel in Japan.*

Serves 10

EQUIPMENT

1	*stand mixer + 2 mixer bowls*
1	*8¼-inch (21-cm) round cake pan, 2 inches (5.5 cm) deep*

—

HONEY SHORTBREAD COOKIES

40 G	*whole-wheat flour*
120 G	*all-purpose flour (T55)*
3.5 G	*baking powder*
0.5 G	*fine sea salt*
50 G	*unsalted butter*
25 G	*honey*
35 G	*demerara sugar*
25 G	*water*

—

CRUST

125 G	*honey shortbread cookies* (SEE ABOVE)
30 G	*speculoos cookies*
55 G	*demerara sugar*
45 G	*unsalted butter*

—

FILLING

485 G	*cream cheese, at room temperature*
65 G	*crème fraîche*
110 G	*superfine sugar, divided*
7 G	*cornstarch*
60 G	*egg yolks (3 yolks from large eggs)*
	finely grated zest of ½ lemon
105 G	*egg whites (from about 3 large eggs)*

Honey shortbread cookies

01.   The day before serving the cheesecake, preheat the oven to 330°F (165°C) and line a baking sheet with parchment paper. Fit the stand mixer with the paddle attachment and sift both flours and the baking powder together into the bowl. Add the salt. Melt the butter, honey, and sugar in a small saucepan and pour into the mixer bowl. Beat on low speed until small balls of dough begin to form, then add the water and beat until the dough comes together.

02.   Turn the dough out onto a lightly floured surface and roll it to a thickness of about ¼ inch (5 mm). Using a sharp knife and ruler, cut the dough into 2-inch (5-cm) squares and place on the prepared baking sheet.

03.   Bake for 15 to 18 minutes.

Cheesecake crust

01.   The day before serving the cheesecake, fit the stand mixer with the paddle attachment and place 125 g of the honey shortbread cookies in the bowl with the speculoos cookies and demerara sugar. In a small saucepan, melt the butter, then pour it into the bowl. Beat on low speed until the butter is evenly distributed and the shortbread cookies are broken up into approximately ½-inch (1-cm) pieces.

02.   Line the base and sides of the cake pan with two pieces of parchment paper cut to fit perfectly inside. Weigh out 250 g of the crust mixture; add it to the prepared pan and spread it across the base. Using a flat object, press down on the crust to ensure even thickness.

Cheesecake filling

01.   The day before serving the cheesecake, fit the stand mixer with the paddle attachment. Place the cream cheese in the bowl and beat on low speed until smooth. Add the crème fraîche and continue beating on low speed until well blended, scraping down the sides of the bowl as needed.

02.   Preheat the oven to 350°F (180°C). In a small bowl, combine 55 g of the sugar with the cornstarch. Place the egg yolks in a separate small bowl and whisk in the sugar-cornstarch mixture, followed by the lemon zest. Add the egg mixture to the cream cheese mixture in five equal quantities, beating until fully incorporated after each addition.

03.   Fit the stand mixer with the whisk attachment and put the second mixer bowl in place. Pour the egg whites into the bowl. With the mixer on medium speed, add the remaining 55 g sugar in three equal quantities. Continue beating until the whites hold stiff peaks. Add the whites to the filling mixture and whisk just until no white streaks remain.

04.   Pour 100 g of water into a glass; using a marker, draw a line on the glass to mark the water level. Pour the water out and dry the glass well. Using a flexible spatula, stir the filling vigorously to incorporate air. To check the density, return the glass you used for weighing the water to the scale and fill the glass up to the marker line with cheesecake filling. To obtain the ideal texture, the filling should weigh between 78 and 80 g. If the filling is too dense, it will be difficult to cook, and the final texture will be heavy. Pour the filling over the crust in the cake pan and smooth the surface using a spatula.

05.   Place the cake pan in a baking dish and pour in enough hot water to come halfway up the sides of the pan. Transfer the baking dish to the oven, close the door, and immediately lower the oven temperature to 285°F (140°C). Bake for 2½ hours, adding more water to the baking dish if necessary (see notes).

06.   Remove the baking dish from the oven and lift the pan out of the hot water. Run a knife blade between the parchment paper and the cheesecake to loosen the edges, and let the cheesecake stand at room temperature for 1 hour. Store it overnight in the refrigerator.

To serve

01.   The next day, turn the cheesecake out of the pan (carefully and briefly submerging the base in hot water will make it easier). Transfer the cake to a serving plate. For perfect slices, heat the blade of a non-serrated knife over a flame before cutting.

NOTES: Although cheesecake may seem simple, it requires a lengthy baking process in a hot-water bath. Monitor the water level in the baking dish closely to ensure it does not dry out.

0
8
4

2 P.M.

Apple Mousse Tartlets

ACTIVE TIME
1 hour 30 minutes

COOKING TIME
15 minutes

I created this pastry while participating in Le Meilleur Pâtissier—Les Professionnels. We had to use apples, and I wanted to explore the fruit's full potential by preparing it in various ways in a single pastry.

Cooking apples sous vide with yuzu and lemon syrup provides fresh notes, while the apple purée in the mousse conveys the fruit's juiciness. The near-liquid consistency of the mousse creates an interesting contrast with the crisp phyllo pastry shell.

Makes 10

EQUIPMENT

1	*mandoline*
1	*instant-read thermometer*
1	*Silikomart SF013 silicone tartlet mold (2 ½ inches at the base, 2 ¾ inches at the rim, ½ inch tall (6 cm × 7 cm × 1.5 cm)*
1	*stand mixer*
1	*sous vide bag*
1	*sous vide cooker*
2	*pastry bags*
10	*3-inch (8-cm) tart rings, ¾ inch (1.5 cm) deep*

—

APPLE CONFIT

1	*Granny Smith apple*
25 G	*freshly squeezed lemon juice*
50 G	*water*
50 G	*superfine sugar*

—

APPLE MOUSSE

60 G	*superfine sugar*
12 G	*water*
30 G	*egg white (1 white from 1 large egg)*
8 G	*gelatin powder*
40 G	*water, heated to 122°F (50°C)*
295 G	*Granny Smith apple purée*
18 G	*Pommeau (apple liqueur), 12% ABV*
145 G	*heavy cream, whipped to stiff peaks*

—

SOUS-VIDE APPLES

135 G	*Golden Delicious apples (about 1 medium apple)*
40 G	*superfine sugar*
2.5 G	*yuzu juice*

Apple confit

01.   Cut the apple into three pieces and remove the core. Using a mandoline, cut the pieces crosswise into very thin (¹⁄₁₆-inch/2-mm) slices.

02.   Combine the lemon juice, water, and sugar in a small saucepan and bring to a boil. Remove the saucepan from the heat and let the syrup cool to 160°F (70°C).

03.   Submerge the apple slices in the syrup for about 30 seconds, then drain them on paper towels. Line the bases of ten of the tartlet mold cavities with three apple slices each, overlapping them slightly (see photo, p. 87).

Apple mousse (see notes)

01.   Prepare an Italian meringue: combine the sugar and water in a small saucepan. Warm until the sugar dissolves and the syrup reaches 239°F (115°C). Meanwhile, fit the stand mixer with the whisk attachment, add the egg white to the bowl, and beat until frothy. With the mixer running on high speed, slowly pour the syrup in a thin stream down the side of the bowl. Beat on high speed until the meringue holds medium peaks, then lower the speed to medium and beat until it has cooled to room temperature.

02.   In a small bowl, dissolve the gelatin powder in the 122°F (50°C) water. In a large bowl, whisk together the apple purée and Pommeau. Pour in one-third of the dissolved gelatin and whisk until well blended, then whisk in the rest. Fold in the whipped cream, followed by the Italian meringue. Spoon the mousse over the apples in the tartlet mold, filling the cavities completely. Place the mold in the freezer for 2 hours before glazing.

Sous-vide apples

01.   Peel and quarter the apple and remove the core. Cut each quarter crosswise into ¼- inch (6-mm) slices and place in a bowl with the sugar and yuzu juice. Stir gently to coat.

02.   Place the mixture in the sous vide bag and seal. Program the sous vide cooker to 195°F (90°C). When the water reaches this temperature, submerge the bag in it and let the apples cook for 5 minutes to let the syrup fully seep into the fruit.

→

"In my opinion, a new recipe or cake can only be called a 'creation' after customers have tried it and expressed their appreciation for it."

FRANGIPANE

60 G   *pastry cream* (P. 170)
140 G   *almond cream* (P. 177)

—

TARTLET SHELLS

   Melted unsalted butter
6   *sheets phyllo dough*

—

ASSEMBLY AND DECORATION

200 G   *pastry cream* (P. 170)
   neutral mirror glaze
   *phyllo dough scraps from
   the bases*

Frangipane

01.   Place the pastry cream in a large bowl and gently stir to loosen it. Using a flexible spatula, fold in the almond cream until the mixture is well blended and smooth. Transfer the frangipane to the pastry bag.

Tartlet shells

01.   Preheat the oven to 330°F (165°C) and place the tart rings on a baking sheet lined with parchment paper. Brush a thin layer of melted butter over one sheet of phyllo dough. Cover with a second sheet and brush with butter. Repeat with the third sheet. Smooth the top with your hand to remove any air.

02.   Layer the 3 remaining sheets of phyllo dough in the same way, separately.

03.   Cut the dough into ten 4½-inch (11-cm) squares, saving the scraps for decoration. Line the tart rings with the dough (see Lining a Tart Ring with Phyllo Dough, p. 178). Pipe 20 g of frangipane onto the base of each tartlet.

04.   Place the phyllo dough scraps on the baking sheet with the tartlet bases and bake for 15 minutes. Let cool completely.

Assembly and decoration

01.   Place the 200 g pastry cream in a pastry bag. Pipe 20 g of pastry cream into each tartlet base, over the frangipane.

02.   Place two sous vide apple slices in each tartlet, pressing down gently to nestle the fruit into the pastry cream.

03.   Place a little mirror glaze in a shallow dish and heat it in the microwave until it reaches 86°F (30°C). Remove the silicone mold from the freezer, turn out the frozen mousse components, and dip them in the mirror glaze with the apple confit slices facing down. Place in the tartlet shells with the apple slices facing up.

04.   Decorate the sides of the mousse with shards of phyllo pastry. Let thaw before serving.

NOTES: As the mousse contains a high percentage of apple purée, make sure the meringue is well whipped. Prepare the mousse quickly and place any excess in the refrigerator immediately, as the purée discolors quickly.

With their tart flavor, Granny Smith apples seem to suit this recipe best.

Coconut Sablés

ACTIVE TIME	RESTING TIME	COOKING TIME
15 minutes	*1 hour*	*18 minutes*

I'll always remember the day I discovered, with wonder, "real" butter in France. Butter is available in Japan, of course, but I didn't realize the difference until I came to Paris. French butter has a rich flavor that fills the mouth and lends a unique taste to pastries. I often create recipes to relive this day, and these coconut sablés are one example.

They have a light texture and almost melt in your mouth before you even chew them. The coconut is discreet and elegant. The secret to these cookies' success lies in the perfect balance between the coconut flavor, the delicate crumbly consistency, and, bien sûr, the unique aroma and flavor of the butter.

Makes 40 cookies

SABLÉ DOUGH

100 G	*unsalted butter, at room temperature*
40 G	*confectioners' sugar*
13 G	*egg yolk (about ½ yolk from 1 large egg)*
1 G	*pure vanilla extract*
100 G	*unsweetened desiccated coconut*
100 G	*pastry flour (T45)*

—

DECORATION

sanding sugar, for coating

Sablé dough

01.   In a large bowl, work together the butter and confectioners' sugar until smooth and creamy. Stir in the egg yolk and vanilla, then incorporate the coconut. Sift in the flour and stir just until well blended.

02.   Divide the dough into two pieces weighing 170 g each and shape them into logs, 12 inches (30 cm) long. Cover the logs with plastic wrap and refrigerate for 1 hour.

Baking

01.   Preheat the oven to 325°F (160°C) and line a baking sheet with parchment paper. Remove the plastic wrap from the logs and roll them in the sanding sugar until evenly coated.

02.   Cut the dough crosswise into ¾-inch (1.5-cm) slices and place on the prepared baking sheet. Bake for 18 minutes.

Fruit Roll

ACTIVE TIME	RESTING TIME	COOKING TIME
45 minutes	*2 hours 10 minutes*	*18 minutes*

We make this fruit roll during Japanese Week, when our Parisian boutique offers a selection of Japanese-style cakes. In Japan, fresh fruit is often used in pastries. I thought the fruit roll would also be delicious in France, where fruits' flavors are especially intense.

Although this type of cake is not traditional in France, people enjoy it because it is made with ingredients readily available at the market. The flavors of the fruits complement each other in perfect harmony. Smiles and good things are universal.

Serves 6

EQUIPMENT

1	*stand mixer + 2 mixer bowls*
1	*instant-read thermometer*
1	*22 × 14-inch (56 × 36-cm) pastry frame*
1	*pastry bag*
1	*½-inch (12-mm) plain tip*

—

"SOUFFLÉ" SPONGE

160 G	*whole milk*
90 G	*unsalted butter*
125 G	*pastry flour (T45)*
6.5 G	*baking powder*
185 G	*egg yolks (about 9 yolks from large eggs)*
405 G	*egg whites (about 13½ whites from large eggs), at room temperature, divided*
180 G	*superfine sugar*
3.5 G	*egg-white powder*

—

WHIPPED CREAM

250 G	*heavy cream, cold*
25 G	*mascarpone, cold*
20 G	*superfine sugar*

—

ASSEMBLY

130 G	*strawberries, all about the same size*
½	*kiwi*
⅓	*mango*
1	*banana*
100 G	*pastry cream (P. 170)*
	snow sugar (non-melting sugar)

"Soufflé" sponge

01.   Preheat the oven to 340°F (170°C) and place the pastry frame on a baking sheet lined with parchment paper. Combine the milk and butter in a small saucepan and bring to a boil. Fit the stand mixer with the whisk attachment and sift the flour and baking powder together into the bowl, then add the hot milk mixture and beat on medium speed until well blended.

02.   Whisk together the egg yolks and 80 g of the egg whites (about 2½ whites) in a bowl set over a saucepan of barely simmering water. Whisking, heat the egg mixture to about 86°F (30°C), then pour it into the mixer bowl with the milk and flour mixture and beat until smooth.

03.   To prepare a meringue, whisk together the sugar and egg-white powder in a bowl until well blended. Place the remaining 325 g egg whites (about 10 whites) in the second mixer bowl and beat until the whites hold medium peaks, then add the sugar mixture and beat until the meringue holds firm peaks (see notes). Immediately fold the meringue into the rest of the batter just until no white streaks remain.

04.   Pour the batter into the pastry frame on the baking sheet and smooth it into an even layer using an offset spatula. Bake for 18 minutes, or until the surface is golden and springs back when lightly touched.

05.   Gently slide a spatula between the frame and the sponge to remove the frame and transfer the sponge to a rack. Let it cool for 10 minutes, then press plastic wrap into the golden surface and let the sponge rest at room temperature for at least 1 hour.

06.   Gently peel off the plastic wrap to remove the sponge's browned surface. Remove the parchment paper and cut the sponge in half horizontally to obtain two approximately 14 x 11-inch (36 × 28-cm) rectangles.

Whipped cream

01. Fit the stand mixer with the whisk attachment and place the cream, mascarpone, and sugar in the bowl. Beat on high speed until the cream holds stiff peaks.

NOTES: To make two fruit rolls, use the second sponge rectangle and double the amount of filling.

To ensure the best texture, make sure the meringue is firm and quickly fold it into the sponge batter just until it is no longer visible. Do not overmix.

Take care not to pull on the sponge when rolling it, as it tears easily.

Assembly and decoration

SEE THE STEP-BY-STEP INSTRUCTIONS ON PAGES 94–95.

→

Step-by-Step

ASSEMBLING THE FRUIT ROLL

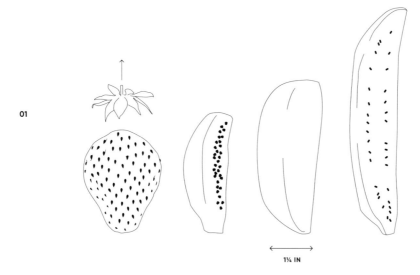

01

1¼ IN

Hull the strawberries. Peel the kiwi and cut it into six pieces lengthwise.

Peel the mango and cut it lengthwise into pieces that are 1¼ inches (3 cm) wide.
Peel the banana, cut it in half lengthwise, and cut off the ends.

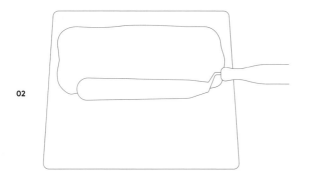

02

Spread a layer of whipped cream over the sponge on the side
where the browned part has been removed.

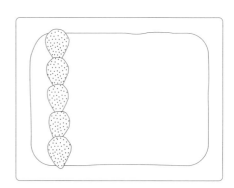

03

Line up several strawberries from end to end along a short edge
of the sponge, leaving a border for rolling.

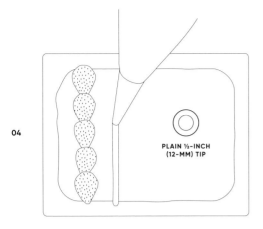

04

Place the 100 g pastry cream in the pastry bag fitted with the ½-inch (12-mm) tip. Pipe a line of cream crosswise across the sponge, about ½ inch (1 cm) from the strawberries.

PLAIN ½-INCH (12-MM) TIP

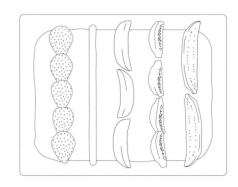

05

Arrange the mango, banana, and kiwi pieces (in that order) in rows spaced about ½ inch (1 cm) apart.

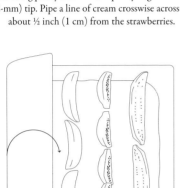

06

Starting at the end with the strawberries, roll up the sponge without pulling on it (see notes). Place it seam-side down on a baking sheet.

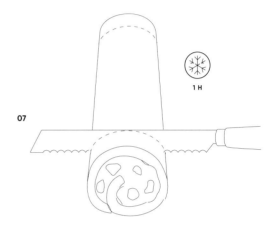

07

1 H

Refrigerate the roll for 1 hour, or until the whipped cream is firm. Before serving, trim 1½ inches (4 cm) off each end so that the roll is 8 inches (20 cm) long.

08

Dust the top with snow sugar.

Lemon Cake

ACTIVE TIME
30 minutes

COOKING TIME
50 minutes

It would be hard to find a pastry shop in France that does not sell cake au citron—lemon loaf cake. It's one of the country's most popular cakes. Many recipes suggest soaking the cake with lemon syrup after it is baked, perhaps because the French enjoy the texture of soaked pastries such as rum baba or coffee-dipped cookies or bread. This method adds lemon flavor but does not necessarily enhance the aroma.

In this recipe, I have tried to emphasize the lemon flavor by using a lemon glaze, which adds a distinct tanginess. The lemon zest in the batter imparts a lemony fragrance, and the glaze seals in the aroma and gives the impression of a whole lemon.

Makes 2 cakes, 480 g each

EQUIPMENT

2	*7 × 6 × 2¾-inch (18 × 16 × 7-cm) loaf pans*
1	*stand mixer*
1	*instant-read thermometer*

—

CAKE BATTER

2	*lemons*
295 G	*superfine sugar*
125 G	*mascarpone*
0.2 G	*fine sea salt (about 1 small pinch)*
210 G	*lightly beaten eggs (about 4 large eggs)*
115 G	*pastry flour (T45)*
115 G	*all-purpose flour (T55)*
8 G	*baking powder*
25 G	*dark rum*
85 G	*unsalted butter*

BAKING

	unsalted butter, softened

—

LEMON GLAZE

25 G	*freshly squeezed lemon juice (use zested lemons from above)*
120 G	*confectioners' sugar*

Lemon cake

01.   Preheat the oven to 325°F (160°C). Grease the loaf pans with butter and dust them with flour. Finely grate the zest of the 2 lemons (set the lemons aside for the glaze). Fit the stand mixer with the whisk attachment and combine the lemon zest and sugar in the bowl. Add the mascarpone and salt and beat until well blended.

02.   Place the eggs in a small bowl set over a saucepan of barely simmering water. Whisking, heat the eggs to 86°F (30°C). With the mixer running on high speed, gradually pour the eggs into the batter. Beat until the sugar has dissolved completely (see notes).

03.   Sift the flours and baking powder together into the bowl and beat on low speed until just incorporated. Mix in the rum. In a small saucepan, melt the butter to 122°F (50°C). Remove the saucepan from the heat. Stir one-fourth of the batter into the melted butter until well blended, then pour this mixture into the mixer bowl with the remaining batter. Stir just until well blended.

Baking and glazing

01.   Place the softened butter in a cone made of parchment paper. Divide the batter between the loaf pans and pipe a line of butter down the center of each lengthwise, from end to end.

02.   Bake for 20 minutes, until the tops begin to dry out and small bubbles appear.

03.   Remove the pans from the oven. Using the tip of a knife, cut a slit down the center of each cake lengthwise, from end to end, to help them expand. Return to the oven and continue to bake for an additional 20 to 25 minutes. Let the cakes cool in the pans for 10 minutes at room temperature, then remove them from the pan and let them cool completely in the refrigerator before glazing.

04.   Preheat the oven to 200°F (100°C). To prepare the lemon glaze, combine the lemon juice and confectioners' sugar in a small saucepan. Heat until the sugar dissolves and the glaze reaches 68°F (20°C). Brush the tops and sides of the cakes with a thin layer of glaze and place them in the oven for 10 minutes.

NOTES: When you add the eggs, be sure to continue beating until there are no sugar particles left at all.

Pistachio-Raspberry Saint-Honoré

ACTIVE TIME
1 hour

RESTING TIME
4 hours

COOKING TIME
50 minutes

Upon my arrival in France, I saw Saint-Honoré cakes everywhere, but I have to admit that I did not find them particularly interesting at the time. Among the traditional French pastries layered with pastry cream, I preferred the Paris-Brest or the millefeuille.

However, I recognized that no French pastry shop would be complete without a Saint-Honoré. So I decided to make a more original version by combining pistachio and raspberry.

Makes 6

EQUIPMENT

1	*3-inch (7.5-cm) round pastry cutter*
	pie weights
1	*1-inch (2.5-cm) round pastry cutter*
4	*pastry bags*
1	*½-inch (12-mm) plain tip*
1	*cream-puff filling tip*
1	*instant-read thermometer*
1	*silicone mold with 1¼-inch (3-cm) half-sphere cavities*
1	*stand mixer*
1	*⅔-inch (15-mm) star tip*

—

PISTACHIO CREAM

4.5 G	*gelatin powder*
22 G	*water, heated to 122°F (50°C)*
445 G	*heavy cream, divided*
65 G	*superfine sugar*
40 G	*pistachio paste*
50 G	*mascarpone*

—

CRAQUELIN COATING

105 G	*unsalted butter, at room temperature*
60 G	*superfine sugar*
135 G	*all-purpose flour (T55)*

—

PUFF PASTRY BASES

120 G	*inverse puff pastry* (P. 172)

—

CRAQUELIN-TOPPED CHOUX PUFFS

	craquelin coating (from above)
	choux pastry (P. 171)

Pistachio cream

01.   In a small bowl, dissolve the gelatin powder in the 122°F (50°C) water. Combine 65 g of the cream with the sugar in a small saucepan and bring to a boil. Remove from the heat and stir in the dissolved gelatin. Place the pistachio paste in a large bowl and gradually whisk in half of the hot liquid until smooth, then whisk in the remaining liquid. Pass the mixture through a fine-mesh sieve into a large bowl.

02.   In a separate large bowl, whisk the mascarpone to loosen it, then whisk in the remaining 380 g cream. Fold into the pistachio-cream mixture, press plastic wrap over the surface, and place in the refrigerator for 3 hours.

Craquelin coating

01.   Stir together the butter, sugar, and flour in a medium bowl until well blended and smooth. Let rest in the refrigerator for 2 hours.

Puff pastry bases

01.   On a lightly floured surface, roll the puff pastry to a thickness of about ¹⁄₁₆ inch (2 mm). Using the 3-inch (7.5-cm) pastry cutter, cut out six disks of dough and place them on a baking sheet lined with parchment paper. Place the baking sheet in the refrigerator for 1 hour.

02.   Preheat the oven to 340°F (170°C). Cut out six 3-inch (7.5-cm) circles of parchment paper and set them on the pastry disks. Top with pie weights. Bake for 25 to 30 minutes. Remove the pie weights and paper, transfer the bases to a rack, and let them cool completely before using.

Craquelin-topped choux puffs

01.   Roll the craquelin coating into a very thin layer (¹⁄₁₆ inch/1 mm) between two sheets of parchment paper. Remove the top piece of parchment paper, then, using the 1-inch (2.5-cm) pastry cutter, cut out eighteen craquelin disks.

02.   Preheat the oven to 340°F (170°C). Place the choux pastry in a pastry bag fitted with the ½-inch (12-mm) tip and pipe out eighteen 1¼-inch (3-cm) round puffs onto a baking sheet. Top each with a craquelin disk. Bake for 20 minutes. Let cool before filling.

→

"I'm often told that my pastries are not very sweet, although using less sugar is not my main objective. Sweetness draws out the flavor of each ingredient, so when the flavors are well-balanced, the sugar itself is less conspicuous."

RASPBERRY PASTRY CREAM

260 G	*pastry cream* (P. 170)*, cooled*
80 G	*heavy cream, whipped to stiff peaks*
60 G	*fresh raspberries, frozen*

—

SUGAR-COATED PISTACHIOS

30	*shelled pistachios (about 10 g)*
50 G	*superfine sugar*
15 G	*water*

—

CHOUX-PUFF CARAMEL

200 G	*superfine sugar*
60 G	*glucose syrup*
40 G	*water*
	caramel coloring, as needed
	cooled craquelin-topped choux puffs (P. 198)

—

DECORATION

60 G	*pistachio praline paste*
6	*fresh raspberries*
	snow sugar (non-melting sugar)

Raspberry pastry cream

01.   Place the pastry cream in a large bowl and whisk in the whipped cream. Place the frozen raspberries in a plastic bag and crush them with a rolling pin to obtain raspberry bits. Stir into the cream. Transfer the cream to a pastry bag fitted with the ½-inch (12-mm) plain tip.

02.   Using the long pointed tip, poke a hole in the bottom center of each choux puff, then fill each generously with raspberry pastry cream.

Sugar-coated pistachios

01.   Plunge the pistachios into a saucepan of boiling water and let them cook for 1 minute, then drain. In a separate small saucepan, warm the sugar and water over medium heat until syrup reaches 239°F (115°C). Add the pistachios.

02.   Stirring continuously with a spatula, cook for 1 to 2 minutes, until the syrup dries out and turns white. Spread the sugar-coated pistachios across a baking sheet and let them cool.

Choux-puff caramel

01.   Combine the superfine sugar, glucose, and water in a medium saucepan and bring to a boil. Add enough caramel coloring to attain the desired color and heat to 340°F (170°C). Submerge the base of the saucepan in a bowl of cold water for 5 seconds to stop the caramelization process. Remove the saucepan and let the caramel cool to 265°F (130°C).

02.   When the caramel reaches 265°F (130°C), pick up the choux puffs one by one with tongs and dip the craquelin-topped side in the caramel to glaze. Place caramel-side down in the cavities of the half-sphere mold to obtain a very smooth finish. Let sit until the caramel has set—check by tapping the base of the mold.

Assembly and decoration

01.   Arrange three caramel-coated choux puffs on top of each puff-pastry disk. Place the pistachio praline paste in a pastry bag and pipe 10 g onto the center of each pastry disk, in the middle of the puffs.

02.   Fit the stand mixer with the whisk attachment and place the chilled pistachio cream in the bowl. Beat until the cream holds stiff peaks, taking care not to overbeat it (see notes). Transfer the whipped pistachio cream to a pastry bag fitted with the ⅔-inch (15-mm) star tip and pipe a generous amount between the choux puffs on the sides and then in the center, forming a small mound on top.

03.   Decorate each Saint-Honoré with 5 sugar-coated pistachios and 1 raspberry with the top dipped in snow sugar.

NOTES: The pistachio cream should be quite firm when assembling the Saint-Honorés, but overbeating it will cause it to separate, and the shape will not hold.

Fig Macarons

ACTIVE TIME
1 hour

RESTING TIME
2 hours

COOKING TIME
30 minutes

Pierre Hermé's influence is evident in this recipe, which shows how much I respect this great pastry chef. This pastry is also my way of expressing my love for the black fig. I still vividly remember the shock to my taste buds when I first tried black figs during a stay in France.

These figs are juicy, fragrant, and honey-sweet. When I returned to Japan, I planted six fig trees in the garden of my pastry shop and soon added fig tarts to my repertoire.

Serves 6

EQUIPMENT

1	*instant-read thermometer*
1	*stand mixer*
3	*pastry bags*
1	*½-inch (12-mm) plain tip*
1	*2½-inch (6.5-cm) round pastry cutter*
1	*refractometer (optional)*

—

MACARON SHELLS

410 G	*superfine sugar*
90 G	*water, at room temperature, divided*
315 G	*egg whites (about 10½ whites from large eggs), at room temperature, divided*
410 G	*almond flour*
410 G	*confectioners' sugar water-soluble purple food coloring, as needed*

—

BLACK FIG JAM

155 G	*black figs*
95 G	*superfine sugar*

—

BUTTERCREAM

120 G	*superfine sugar*
25 G	*water*
60 G	*egg whites (2 whites from large eggs)*
375 G	*unsalted butter, at room temperature*

⟶

Macaron shells

01.   Prepare an Italian meringue: combine the superfine sugar with 80 g of the water in a large saucepan. Warm until the sugar dissolves and the syrup reaches 239°F (115°C). Meanwhile, fit the stand mixer with the whisk attachment, add 150 g of the egg whites (5 whites) to the bowl, and beat until the whites are frothy. With the mixer running on high speed, slowly pour the syrup in a thin stream down the side of the bowl. Beat on high speed until the meringue holds medium peaks, then lower the speed to medium and beat until it has cooled to room temperature.

02.   Sift the almond flour and confectioners' sugar together into a large bowl. In a separate large bowl, combine the remaining 165 g egg whites (about 5 ½ whites) with the remaining 10 g water. Stir in the almond flour-confectioners' sugar mixture until well blended and smooth.

03.   Using a flexible spatula, fold in the Italian meringue, mashing it gently as you go. Add a small amount of purple food coloring and continue to fold until evenly incorporated. Add more color if necessary. Transfer the batter to a pastry bag fitted with the plain ½-inch (12-mm) tip.

04.   Using the pastry cutter, draw twelve circles on a sheet of parchment paper as a template for piping the macaron shells. Turn the paper over, place it on a baking sheet, and pipe out batter to fill the circles. Gently tap the baking sheet against a work surface to distribute the batter more evenly. Let dry at room temperature for about 2 hours.

05.   Preheat the oven to 300°F (150°C). Bake the macaron shells for 4 minutes, then open the oven door slightly, lower the temperature to 250°F (120°C), and bake with the door open for 2 minutes. Close the oven door and continue to bake for 15 to 20 minutes, until the shells can be easily lifted off the parchment paper. Remove from the oven and let cool completely on the baking sheet.

Black fig jam

01.   Cut the figs into six pieces each, place them in a medium saucepan with the sugar, and mash them with a fork. Bring the mixture to a boil. If you have a refractometer, use it to check the sugar content. Continue to cook until the mixture reaches 56° Brix. If you do not have a refractometer, let the mixture cook at a boil for 1 minute. Transfer the jam to a bowl, press plastic wrap over the surface, and let cool in the refrigerator.

Buttercream

01.   Prepare an Italian meringue: combine the superfine sugar and water in a large saucepan. Warm until the sugar dissolves and the syrup reaches 239°F (115°C). Meanwhile, fit the stand mixer with the whisk attachment, place the egg whites in the bowl, and beat until the whites are frothy. With the mixer running on high speed, gradually pour the syrup in a thin stream down the side of the bowl. Beat on high speed until the meringue holds medium peaks, then lower the speed to medium and beat until it has cooled to room temperature.

02.   Add the butter and beat until well combined and smooth. Keep at room temperature.

⟶

> **"My dream is that, thirty years from now, my contributions will be regarded as part of the classic French pastry repertoire."**

CARAMEL SAUCE

185 G *superfine sugar*
165 G *heavy cream*

—

CARAMEL MOUSSELINE CREAM

200 g *pastry cream* (P. 170)
100 g *caramel sauce (from above)*
       finely grated zest of 1 orange
155 g *buttercream* (P. 102), *at room*
       temperature

—

ASSEMBLY

6   *ripe black figs*
       neutral mirror glaze

Caramel sauce

01.   In a large heavy saucepan, heat the sugar until it melts and begins to caramelize. Gently swirl the pan. As soon as fine bubbles appear on the surface, remove from the heat. Stirring continuously, very gradually pour in the cream. Stir until well blended. Strain the sauce through a fine-mesh sieve into a bowl and set it over a larger bowl filled with ice water. Leave the bowl over the ice water, stirring often, until the sauce has cooled completely.

Caramel mousseline cream

01.   Place the pastry cream in a large bowl and whisk gently to loosen it, then whisk in the caramel sauce and orange zest. Set the bowl over a saucepan of barely simmering water and heat until the mixture reaches 79°F (26°C), then gently incorporate the buttercream. Take care not to overmix, as the cream could separate (see notes). Transfer the caramel mousseline cream to a pastry bag fitted with the ½-inch (12-mm) tip.

Assembly and baking

SEE THE STEP-BY-STEP INSTRUCTIONS ON PAGE 105.

NOTES: When mixing the buttercream, be sure to respect the temperature given to ensure the pastry cream and butter come together.

Step-by-Step

ASSEMBLING THE MACARONS

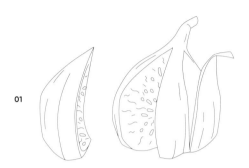

01

Peel the figs and cut each lengthwise into eight equal pieces.

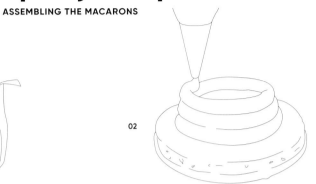

02

½-INCH (12-MM)
PLAIN TIP

Take one macaron shell and pipe out three rings of caramel mousseline cream, one on top of the other, leaving a hole in the center and a border around the outside edge.

03

Transfer the fig jam to a pastry bag without a tip. Pipe 10 g of jam into the center of the cream ring.

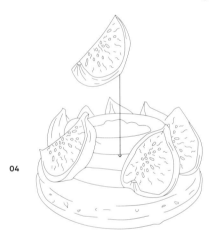

04

Arrange the fig pieces around the cream.

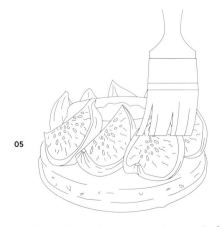

05

Brush a thin layer of neutral mirror glaze over the figs.

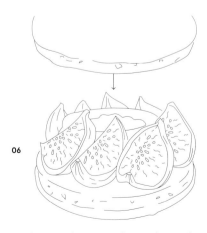

06

Cover the jam in the center with caramel mousseline cream and top with a second macaron shell.

Maple Cake

ACTIVE TIME
30 minutes

COOKING TIME
45 minutes

*In my opinion, maple sugar deserves to be better known in France.
Once you get used to the flavor, you really acquire a taste for it!
Deeper in flavor than maple syrup, maple sugar provides contrast to the light
texture of this cake. I call it a loaf cake because of the shape of the mold,
but it's actually a Genoise sponge.*

Makes 2 cakes, 330 g each

EQUIPMENT

2	*7 × 6 × 2¾-inch (18 × 16 × 7-cm) loaf pans*
1	*stand mixer*
1	*instant-read thermometer*

—

CAKE BATTER

135 G	*almond paste*
60 G	*maple sugar*
60 G	*demerara sugar*
170 G	*lightly beaten eggs (from about 3 large eggs)*
125 G	*unsalted butter*
60 G	*maple syrup*
70 G	*pastry flour (T45)*
70 G	*all-purpose flour (T55)*
3 G	*baking powder*

GLAZE

120 G	*confectioners' sugar*
25 G	*water*

Cake batter

01.   Preheat the oven to 325°F (160°C). Grease the loaf pans with butter and dust them with flour. Fit the stand mixer with the whisk attachment. Briefly heat the almond paste in the microwave to soften it, then place it in the mixer bowl. Add the maple sugar and demerara sugar and beat until well blended.

02.   Place the eggs in a small bowl set over a saucepan of barely simmering water. Whisking, heat the eggs to 86°F (30°C). Add one-fifth of the warmed eggs to the mixer bowl and beat on high speed until a firm paste forms. If you add too much egg at once, the almond paste will turn lumpy.

03.   With the mixer running on high speed, add the remaining eggs in two equal quantities, scraping down the sides of the bowl after each addition. Beat until the mixture is pale and airy, then lower the speed to medium and beat for an additional 3 minutes. This will stabilize the mixture and ensure an even consistency.

04.   Combine the butter and maple syrup in a saucepan and heat to 122°F (50°C), stirring. Remove the saucepan from the heat and stir in one-third of the egg-sugar mixture. Sift both flours and the baking powder together into the mixer bowl with the egg-sugar mixture and fold in just until no streaks remain. Gently fold in the butter mixture, taking care not to overmix.

Baking and glazing

01.   Divide the batter between the loaf pans and bake for 35 minutes. After baking, the cake will stick to the sides of the pan, so gently slide a knife blade between the sides of the cake and the pans to make them easier to turn out. Let the cakes cool in the pans for 10 minutes, then turn them out and let them cool completely in the refrigerator before glazing.

02.   Preheat the oven to 200°F (100°C). To prepare the glaze, stir together the confectioners' sugar and water in a small bowl until smooth. Brush the tops and sides of the cakes with a thin layer of glaze and place them in the oven for 10 minutes.

NOTES: Heating the eggs and the butter-maple syrup mixture makes it easier to mix them into the other ingredients. As a result, the cakes will rise better when baked.

Antharès

ACTIVE TIME	RESTING TIME	COOKING TIME
1 hour 15 minutes	*12 hours + 3 hours*	*18 minutes*

In Japan, strawberries are mainly grown in greenhouses, and are now considered a winter fruit.
They are also very sweet; the Japanese generally seek to produce ever-sweeter varieties. But when used in baking, these strawberries
often turn insipid. Seasonal French strawberries have a more pronounced acidity, and the chance to work with them is a new
experience entirely, precious for a pastry chef. I like to pair the berries with citrus to accentuate their tartness.

Serves 6

EQUIPMENT

1	*refractometer (optional)*
1	*7-inch (18-cm) ring mold*
3	*pastry bags*
1	*½-inch (12-mm) plain tip*
1	*immersion blender (optional)*
1	*22 × 14-inch (56 × 36-cm) pastry frame*
1	*stand mixer + 2 mixer bowls*
1	*instant-read thermometer*
1	*7-inch (18-cm) round pastry cutter*
1	*2½-inch (6-cm) round pastry cutter*
1	*6-inch (16-cm) ring mold*

—

STRAWBERRY MARSHMALLOW

6 G	*gelatin powder*
30 G	*water, heated to 122°F (50°C)*
55 G	*strawberry purée*
65 G	*invert sugar (Trimoline)*
85 G	*superfine sugar*
13 G	*water*
0.6 G	*citric acid (optional)*
	snow sugar (non-melting sugar)

—

STRAWBERRY COMPOTE

115 G	*medium strawberries, preferably Gariguette*
50 G	*freshly squeezed lime juice*
85 G	*superfine sugar*
2.5 G	*gelatin powder*
13 G	*water, heated to 122°F (50°C)*

—

"SOUFFLÉ" SPONGE

160 G	*whole milk*
90 G	*unsalted butter*
125 G	*pastry flour (T45)*
6.5 G	*baking powder*
185 G	*egg yolks (about 9 yolks from large eggs)*
405 G	*egg whites (about 13½ whites from large eggs), at room temperature, divided*
180 G	*superfine sugar*
3.5 G	*egg white powder*

Strawberry marshmallow

01.　The day before preparing the Antharès, dissolve the gelatin powder in the 122°F (50°C) water in a small bowl. Combine the strawberry purée, invert sugar, superfine sugar, and water in a saucepan, then stir in the dissolved gelatin. Bring the mixture to a boil. If you have a refractometer, use it to check the sugar content. Continue to cook until the mixture reaches 67° Brix. If you do not have a refractometer, let the mixture boil for 10 minutes. Remove from the heat and stir in the citric acid, if using. Fit the stand mixer with the paddle attachment, transfer the marshmallow mixture to the bowl, and beat on high speed until it is stiff and does not fall from the whisk when lifted. Transfer to a pastry bag fitted with the ½-inch (12-mm) tip.

02.　Draw an 8-inch (20-cm) circle on a sheet of parchment paper. Turn the paper over, place it on a baking sheet, and dust it with snow sugar. Pipe out a rope of the marshmallow mixture around the 8-inch (20-cm) circle, without connecting the ends. Let the marshmallow dry overnight at room temperature. The next day, dust the marshmallow with snow sugar.

Strawberry compote

01.　The next day, hull the strawberries and freeze them whole. Once they are completely frozen, place them in a bowl, stir in the lime juice and sugar, and let thaw at room temperature.

02.　In a small bowl, dissolve the gelatin powder in the 122°F (50°C) water. Pour the thawed strawberry mixture into a medium saucepan and bring to a boil. Remove from the heat and gently stir in the dissolved gelatin using a flexible spatula. Transfer to a bowl, press plastic wrap over the surface, and refrigerate for at least 3 hours, or until well chilled.

03.　Remove six pieces of strawberry from the compote and arrange them around the base of the 7-inch (18-cm) ring mold. Place the mold in the refrigerator to firm up the gelatin. If you see other pieces of strawberry in the compote, process it briefly with an immersion blender.

"Soufflé" sponge

01.　Preheat the oven to 340°F (170°C) and place the pastry frame on a baking sheet lined with parchment paper. Combine the milk and butter in a saucepan and bring to a boil. Fit the stand mixer with the whisk attachment and sift the flour and baking powder together into the bowl, then add the hot milk mixture and beat on medium speed until well blended.

02.　Whisk together the egg yolks and 80 g of the egg whites (about 2½ whites) in a bowl set over a saucepan of barely simmering water. Whisking, heat the egg mixture to about 86°F (30°C), then pour it into the mixer bowl with the milk and flour mixture and beat until smooth.

03.　To prepare a meringue, whisk together the sugar and egg white powder in a bowl until well blended. Place the remaining 325 g egg whites (about 10 whites) in the second mixer bowl and beat until the whites hold medium peaks, then add the sugar mixture and beat until the meringue holds firm peaks. Immediately fold the meringue into the rest of the batter just until no white streaks remain.

04.　Pour the batter into the pastry frame on the baking sheet and smooth it into an even layer using an offset spatula. Bake for 18 minutes, or until the surface is golden and springs back when lightly touched.

05.　Gently slide a spatula between the frame and the sponge to remove the frame and transfer the sponge to a rack. Let it cool for 10 minutes, then press plastic wrap over the browned surface and let the sponge rest at room temperature for at least 1 hour.

06.　After this resting time, gently peel off the plastic wrap to remove the browned layer. To obtain a sponge ring the same size as the larger ring mold, cut out a 7-inch (18-cm) sponge disk using the larger pastry cutter, then cut out the center of the disk using the 2½-inch (6-cm) cutter.

→

LIME CREAM

2 G   *gelatin powder*

10 G   *water, heated to 122°F (50°C)*

70 G   *lime purée*

70 G   *freshly squeezed lime juice finely grated zest of ⅓ lime*

90 G   *superfine sugar*

9 G   *cornstarch*

75 G   *lightly beaten eggs (1½ large eggs)*

70 G   *egg yolks (about 3½ yolks from large eggs)*

75 G   *unsalted butter, at room temperature*

—

STRAWBERRY MOUSSE

6 G   *gelatin powder*

30 G   *water, heated to 122°F (50°C)*

125 G   *strawberry purée*

10 G   *freshly squeezed lime juice*

20 G   *strawberry compote* (P. 108)

25 G   *superfine sugar*

5 G   *water*

20 G   *egg white (about ⅔ white from 1 large egg)*

150 G   *heavy cream, whipped to medium peaks*

10 G   *mascarpone*

—

STRAWBERRY GLAZE

60 G   *strawberry purée*

300 G   *neutral mirror glaze*

—

DECORATION

finely grated zest of 1 lime
Fresh strawberries, preferably Gariguette

Lime cream

01.　In a small bowl, dissolve the gelatin powder in the 122°F (50°C) water. Combine the lime purée, juice, and zest in a medium saucepan and bring to a boil. In a separate small bowl, whisk together the sugar and cornstarch. In a medium bowl, whisk together the eggs and egg yolks, then whisk in the sugar-cornstarch mixture. Whisking continuously, gradually pour one-third of the hot lime mixture into the egg mixture, then pour everything back into the saucepan. Stirring continuously, cook until the mixture reaches 172°F (78°C). Remove the saucepan from the heat and stir in the butter and dissolved gelatin.

02.　Strain the lime cream through a fine-mesh sieve into a bowl and set it over a larger bowl filled with ice water to cool it quickly. Leave the bowl over ice water, stirring often, until the cream reaches 43°F (6°C). Transfer the lime cream to a pastry bag and pipe 300 g of it into the 6-inch (16-cm) ring mold. Place in the freezer for 1 hour, or until the cream has set and the surface has hardened.

03.　Once the lime cream has set, place 60 g of the strawberry compote in a pastry bag and pipe it over the cream in the mold. If the compote is too firm for piping, place it in a bowl and set it over a saucepan of barely simmering water for a few seconds to loosen it. Return the mold to the freezer for 1 hour to set.

Strawberry mousse

01.　In a medium bowl, dissolve the gelatin powder in the 122°F (50°C) water. In a large bowl, combine the strawberry purée and lime juice. Place the 20 g strawberry compote in a bowl set over a saucepan of barely simmering water for a few seconds until liquefied 54°F–59°F (12°C–15 °C), then whisk it into the strawberry purée mixture. Whisk one-fourth of this mixture into the dissolved gelatin, then return to the large bowl and whisk until well blended.

02.　Prepare an Italian meringue: combine the superfine sugar and 5 g of water in a saucepan. Warm until the sugar dissolves and the syrup reaches 239°F (115°C). Meanwhile, place the egg white in the bowl of the stand mixer fitted with the whisk attachment and beat until the white is frothy. With the mixer running on high speed, slowly pour the syrup in a thin stream down the side of the bowl. Beat on high speed until the meringue holds medium peaks, then lower the speed to medium and beat until it has cooled to room temperature.

03.　Place the whipped cream in a medium bowl and fold in the mascarpone. Fold this whipped cream into the strawberry-lime mixture until well blended, then fold in the Italian meringue.

04.　Transfer the mousse to a pastry bag and pipe about 350 g into the 7-inch (18-cm) ring mold over the strawberry pieces, or enough to fill the mold three-fourths full. Nestle the frozen lime cream ring into the center of the mousse, then add a little more mousse to cover and smooth it over well. Cover with the "soufflé" sponge and place the ring in the freezer until the mousse is firm and does not move when you touch the center of the sponge.

Strawberry glaze

01.　Combine the strawberry purée and mirror glaze in a large saucepan and heat to 86°F (30°C).

Assembly and decoration

01.　Remove the mold from the freezer and turn the gâteau out onto a rack. Pour the strawberry glaze over it until it is well-coated.

02.　Carefully transfer the gâteau to a serving plate and wrap the marshmallow rope around the base.

03.　Sprinkle the top with lime zest and fill the center with halved strawberries.

NOTES: The tangy lime cream hidden inside the strawberry mousse balances the sweetness of the latter, while the strawberry compote enhances the fruit's retronasal impact. Mousse is often considered bland, but the lime cream in this recipe makes the flavor more complex.

3 Rue de Mirbel, Paris 5th Arrondissement – 4:40 p.m.

CHAP. 5

4 p.m.

4 P.M.

Breteuil Sablés

ACTIVE TIME
20 minutes

RESTING TIME
12 hours

COOKING TIME
15 minutes

*Some cookies seem to have been created solely for enjoying the flavors of butter and flour,
and Breteuil sablés fall squarely into this category. I made these cookies when I was in Japan,
but when I began using local ingredients in France, they of course became more flavorsome.*

*When Japanese pâtissiers visit me in France, I have them taste these cookies
so they can experience French flour and butter.*

Makes 18 sablés

EQUIPMENT

1   *2 ½-in (6 cm) round
or scalloped pastry cutter*

—

SABLÉ DOUGH

50 G   *unsalted butter,
at room temperature*
50 G   *superfine sugar*
0.7 G   *fine sea salt*
20 G   *whole milk*
100 G   *pastry flour (T45)*
15 G   *almond flour*
1 G   *baking powder*

—

DECORATION

sanding sugar

Sablé dough

01.   The day before baking, combine the butter, sugar,
and salt in a bowl. Gradually add the milk.

02.   Sift together the flour, almond flour, and baking
powder, then stir it into the butter mixture until combined.

03.   Gather the dough into a ball and place it in a plastic
bag. Let rest overnight in the refrigerator.

Cutting out and baking

01.   Preheat the oven to 340°F (170°C).

02.   Roll the dough to a thickness of about ¼ inch (5 mm).

03.   Grease a baking sheet with butter. Cut out the sablés,
sprinkle them with sanding sugar on both sides, and place
them on the baking sheet.

04.   Bake for 15 minutes.

NOTES: This recipe could not be any simpler in terms of
flavor; its originality lies in the texture. The sprinkling of
sugar on each cookie creates a "sandy" sensation, and melts
immediately in your mouth.

Lemon Tart

ACTIVE TIME	RESTING TIME	COOKING TIME
45 minutes	*3 hours*	*20 minutes*

My shop sold lemon tarts from its opening day, and since then, I have continued to make them, adding small changes in the details. Right now, for example, they are garnished with lemon confit. There is no "all-time" best recipe, only recipes that are right for the moment.

Lemon tarts have taught me valuable lessons precisely because I make them every day: an idea arises after making the same thing a thousand times over—and another after making it two thousand times.

Serves 6 to 8

EQUIPMENT

1	*stand mixer*
1	*8-inch (20-cm) round tart ring, ¾ inch (2 cm) deep*
1	*pastry bag fitted with a ⅒-inch (3-mm) plain tip*
1	*instant-read thermometer*
1	*kitchen blowtorch*

—

105 G	*sweet shortcrust pastry* (P. 176)

—

LEMON FILLING

85 G	*lemon purée*
35 G	*freshly squeezed lemon juice finely grated zest of ½ lemon*
65 G	*eggs (about 1 ¼ eggs)*
60 G	*egg yolks (about 3 yolks from large eggs)*
80 G	*superfine sugar*
8 G	*cornstarch*
65 G	*unsalted butter*

—

ITALIAN MERINGUE

90 G	*superfine sugar*
18 G	*water*
60 G	*egg whites (about from 3 large eggs)*

—

DECORATION

lemon confit, cut into pieces

Sweet shortcrust pastry

01.   Preheat the oven to 330°F (165°C).

02.   Roll the dough to a thickness of about ⅒ inch (2 mm). Cut out a 14-inch (25-cm) circle. Lay the dough over the ring and gently tuck it into the corners and against the sides. Prick the dough with a fork.

03.   Run the blade of a sharp knife along the top edge of the tart ring to trim the crust and obtain a clean edge. Bake for 18 to 20 minutes.

Lemon filling

01.   In a saucepan, bring the lemon purée, juice, and zest to a boil. In a separate bowl, combine the whole eggs, yolks, sugar, and cornstarch. Mix well.

02.   Add a third of the hot liquid into the bowl and mix well. Pour this mixture back into the saucepan and cook over medium heat until it reaches 172°F (78°C).

03.   Remove from the heat and stir in the butter. Strain through a fine-mesh sieve. Let cool at 43°F (6°C) in a bowl filled with ice cubes. Let rest in the refrigerator for 3 hours.

Italian meringue

01.   To prepare an Italian meringue, heat the sugar and water in a saucepan until the syrup reaches 239°F (115°C). Fit the stand mixer with the whisk attachment and place the egg whites in the bowl. Whisk until soft peaks form. Gradually add the syrup, slowly pouring it in a thin stream down the side of the bowl. Beat on high until stiff peaks form. Reduce speed to medium and continue beating until the mixture cools to room temperature. Using a flexible spatula, fill the pastry bag fitted with a plain ⅒-inch (3-mm) tip.

Assembly and decoration

SEE THE STEP-BY-STEP INSTRUCTIONS ON PAGE 119.

→

NOTES: If you can't find lemon purée, you can replace it with lemon juice and the zest of one lemon.

For this recipe, I use a traditional lemon filling, without the addition of gelatin. Although gelatin creates a smoother texture, it simply cannot compare to the creaminess of eggs and butter.

Step-by-Step

**ASSEMBLING AND PIPING
THE LEMON TART**

01

Pour the lemon filling into the crust.

02

Smooth the surface with a cake spatula.

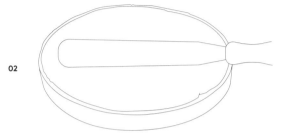

**PASTRY BAG FITTED WITH A
¹⁄₁₀-INCH (3-MM) PLAIN TIP**

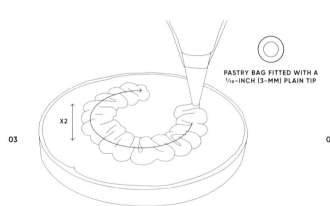

03

Using a small left-to-right zigzag movement, pipe a first ring of meringue in the center of the tart. Pipe a second ring directly on top of the first ring using the same zigzag motion.

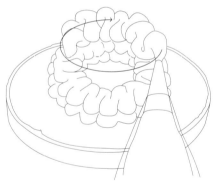

04

Add the last ring of meringue by making small movements from left to right and top to bottom to form small clouds of stacked meringue.

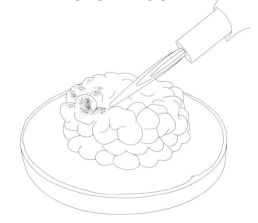

05

Lightly brown the meringue with the kitchen blowtorch.

06

Arrange the pieces of lemon confit around the meringue.

Hazelnut Financiers

ACTIVE TIME	RESTING TIME	COOKING TIME
30 minutes	*2 hours*	*18 minutes*

These financiers celebrate the delightful taste of hazelnuts, which I discovered in France. Their bright fragrance and intense flavor inspired me to create a recipe that would show them off.

I added Piedmont hazelnuts to the ingredients list, along with natural hazelnut flour, including the nut skins. My goal was to bring out the nut's fragrance and highlight its sweetness.

Makes 10

EQUIPMENT

1	*instant-read thermometer*
1	*silicone financier mold, cavities 4 ¾ inches long × 1 ½ inches high x 1 inch deep (12 × 4 cm × 2.5 cm)*

—

FINANCIER BATTER

30 G	*shelled hazelnuts*
120 G	*unsalted butter*
180 G	*egg whites (about 6 whites from large eggs)*
180 G	*confectioners' sugar*
4 G	*fleur de sel*
120 G	*hazelnut flour*
60 G	*all-purpose flour (T55)*

Financier batter

01.   Preheat the oven to 340°F (170°C). Spread the hazelnuts on a baking sheet and roast them for 10 minutes.

02.   Prepare brown butter in a saucepan: melt the butter over low heat and cook until it turns a light golden brown. Strain through a fine-mesh sieve into a bowl.

03.   In another bowl, whisk together the egg whites, confectioners' sugar, and fleur de sel. Heat this mixture in a small bowl set over a saucepan of barely simmering water until it reaches 104 °F (40 °C).

04.   Sift together both flours. Coarsely chop the toasted hazelnuts. Add the flours, chopped hazelnuts, and brown butter to the egg white mixture. Mix well with a spatula to emulsify the batter. Let rest at room temperature for 2 hours. During this time, the batter will release air bubbles, leading to a more stable baking.

05.   Preheat an oven to 340°F (170°C). Place the financier mold on a baking sheet. Lightly grease the molds with butter and fill to the top with batter. Bake in the preheated oven for 15 to 18 minutes, until golden.

NOTES: Our financier contains pieces of hazelnut and has a relatively high salt content to accentuate the flavor contrasts. I also use a mold that is deeper than traditional financier molds to create height and, as a result, achieve a crispy exterior and soft interior.

I suggest serving them slightly cooled, because that is when they are at their best—hence the advantage of making them at home.

Lemon Paris-Brest

ACTIVE TIME
45 minutes

COOKING TIME
1 hour 20 minutes

*The Paris-Brest is one of the traditional pastries—dense and substantial—
that I have worked on. My cakes are usually described as lighter and less
sweet than the original recipes, but this impression is usually a result
of elements that counterbalance the fat and sugar, such as citrus.*

*Making "light" cakes is not my objective. For this one, rather than
arbitrarily reducing the sugar or butter, I tried to bring out flavor nuances
by adding lemon. The fat enhances the taste of the lemon, which in turn
helps to reduce the heaviness of the fat.*

Serves 8

EQUIPMENT

1	*7-inch (18-cm) tart ring*
1	*6-inch (15-cm) tart ring*
1	*⅔-inch (15-mm) star or flower tip (PF16)*
1	*⅓-inch (8-mm) star tip*
1	*silicone baking mat*
1	*decorating comb with ⅕-inch (5-mm) teeth*
1	*stand mixer*

—

CHOUX PASTRY

700 G	*choux pastry (P. 171)*
	unsalted butter, for greasing
	all-purpose flour, for marking sheet
	slivered almonds

—

LEMON PRALINE CREAM

165 G	*unsalted butter, at room temperature*
350 G	*pastry cream (P. 170)*
125 G	*almond praline paste*
125 G	*hazelnut praline paste*
	zest from ⅓ lemon

—

ASSEMBLY

300 G	*pastry cream (P. 170)*
110 G	*hazelnut praline paste*
	snow sugar (non-melting sugar)

Choux pastry

01.   Preheat the oven to 345°F (175°C).

02.   Grease a baking sheet with butter. To help pipe the choux pastry, dip the 7-inch (18-cm) tart ring in flour and use it to make a mark on the baking sheet.

03.   Using a pastry bag fitted with the ⅔-inch (15-mm) star or flower tip, pipe the choux pastry around the rim of the circle. Then make another ring of dough inside the first. Pipe a final ring on top of the other two. Sprinkle with slivered almonds and bake for 45 minutes.

04.   To make the interior ring of the Paris-Brest, pipe two layers of dough 6 inches in diameter. Bake them at 345°F (175°C) for 20 minutes.

05.   To make decorations, delicately spread about 100 g of choux pastry on a silicone baking mat with an offset spatula. Draw the decorating comb over the dough to form batons. Bake at 320°F (160 °C) for 12 to 15 minutes, until they are a rich golden color.

Lemon praline cream

01.   Fit the stand mixer with the whisk attachment, and place the softened butter, pastry cream, both praline pastes, and lemon zest in the bowl.

02.   Whisk until the mixture pales in color, then transfer it to a pastry bag fitted with the ⅓-inch (8-mm) star tip.

Assembling and decoration

SEE THE STEP-BY-STEP INSTRUCTIONS ON PAGES 124–125.

NOTES: Be sure to shape the choux pastry when it is still warm; it is entirely different when it is cold.

Step-by-Step

ASSEMBLING THE PARIS-BREST

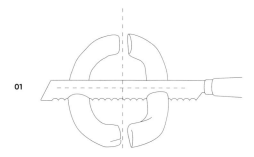

01

Cut the 6-inch (15-cm) pastry ring into four pieces.

02

Fill each piece with pastry cream.

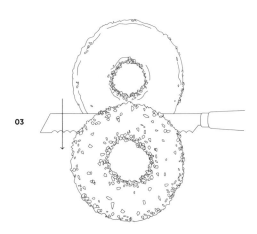

03

Using a serrated knife, cut the 7-inch (18-cm)
pastry ring in half horizontally.

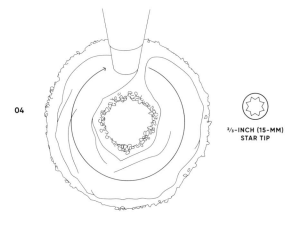

04

⅔-INCH (15-MM)
STAR TIP

Fill the bottom half of the ring with
lemon praline cream.

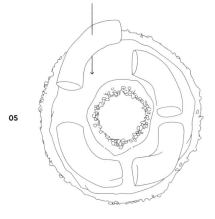

05

Place the filled pieces of the pastry ring on top.

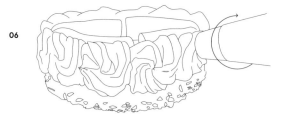

06

Pipe rosettes of lemon praline cream on the outside,
slightly exceeding the height of the inner ring.

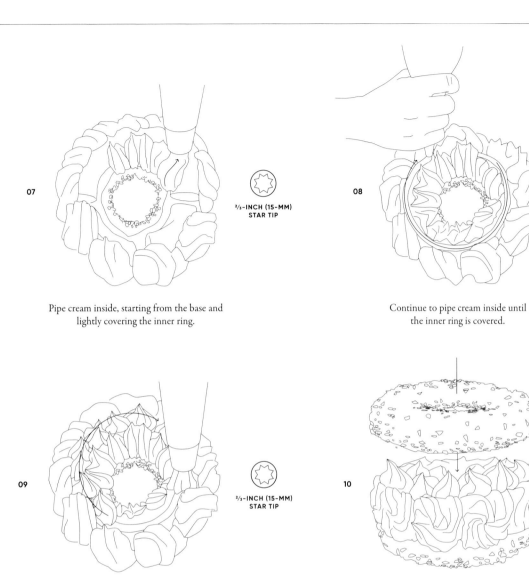

07

⅔-INCH (15-MM) STAR TIP

Pipe cream inside, starting from the base and lightly covering the inner ring.

08

Continue to pipe cream inside until the inner ring is covered.

09

⅔-INCH (15-MM) STAR TIP

Pipe a layer of hazelnut praline paste on the 6-inch (15-cm) ring of choux pastry, then cover it with a layer of piped lemon praline cream balls.

10

Place the other half of the pastry ring on top.

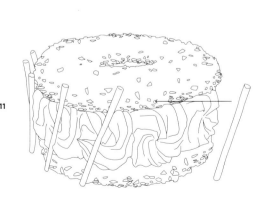

11

Place 3-inch (8-cm) pastry batons on the cream around the Paris-Brest.

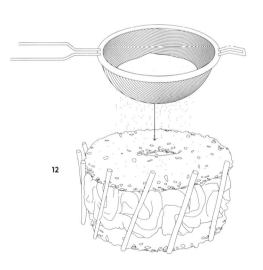

12

Use a fine-mesh sieve to dust the cake with snow sugar.

Chocolate and Coffee Éclairs

ACTIVE TIME
1 hour

RESTING TIME
2 hours

COOKING TIME
25 minutes

*French people grow up eating éclairs, so it is extremely difficult to win them over with this pastry.
When I came to France for the first time, at the age of twenty, I noticed that every bakery
sold chocolate and coffee éclairs, so I insisted on serving them in our shop from the very beginning.
For the coffee éclair, I intentionally use standard coffee, which reminds our clients of the
éclairs they ate as children.*

*For the chocolate version, I did not try to be original or surprising—I simply wanted to recreate
the comforting and relatable flavor of the traditional éclair that everyone is familiar with.*

Makes 12 éclairs
(6 chocolate, 6 coffee)

EQUIPMENT

3	*pastry bags*
1	*offset spatula*
1	*⅔-inch (18 mm) petit-four tip (PF16)*
2	*guitar sheets*

—

400 G	*choux pastry* (P. 171)

—

CRAQUELIN

105 G	*unsalted butter, at room temperature*
60 G	*superfine sugar*
135 G	*all-purpose flour (T55)*

CHOCOLATE CRAQUELIN

105 G	*unsalted butter*
60 G	*superfine sugar*
120 G	*all-purpose flour (T55)*
15 G	*unsweetened cocoa powder*

—

CHOCOLATE CREAM

295 G	*pastry cream* (P. 170), *warm*
90 G	*Valrhona® dark chocolate Guanaja, 70% cacao, melted*
40 G	*mascarpone*

—

COFFEE CREAM

360 G	*pastry cream* (P. 170), *cooled*
40 G	*mascarpone*
17 G	*Trablit coffee extract*
3 G	*instant coffee powder*

—

DECORATIVE
CHOCOLATE LAYER

300 G	*dark chocolate*
300 G	*milk chocolate*

Craquelin and chocolate craquelin

01.   Combine the softened butter, sugar, flour, and cocoa powder (for the chocolate craquelin) in a bowl. Let rest in the refrigerator for 2 hours.

Chocolate pastry cream

01.   Place the warm pastry cream in a large bowl. Add the melted chocolate, and whisk until emulsified. Let cool completely, then fold in the mascarpone. Transfer to a pastry bag.

Coffee pastry cream

01.   Place the cooled pastry cream in a large bowl. Gently fold in the mascarpone, coffee extract, and instant coffee. Transfer to a pastry bag.

Chocolate strips

01.   Using your method of choice, temper the dark and milk chocolates separately (see Tempering Chocolate, pp. 180–181). Using the offset spatula, spread the tempered chocolate into a thin layer on the guitar sheets.

02.   When the chocolate has cooled slightly and hardened, use a sharp knife to cut 6 strips of dark chocolate and 6 strips of milk chocolate, each measuring 1 ¼ × 6 ⅓ inch (3 × 16 cm).

Assembly and decoration

01.   Preheat the oven to 345 °F (175 °C).

02.   On a work surface spread the craquelin dough in a ¹⁄₁₆-inch (2-mm) layer. Using a sharp knife, cut 12 rectangles each measuring 1 ¼ × 6 inch (3 × 15 cm).

03.   Fit one of the pastry bags with the PF16 tip and fill it with choux pastry. Pipe 12 éclairs 6 inches (15 cm) long.

04.   Top each éclair with a rectangle of craquelin. Bake for 25 minutes. Let cool completely on a rack.

05.   Using a serrated knife, cut a small rectangle out of the top center of each éclair. Generously fill each éclair—half with the chocolate cream, and half with the coffee cream.

06.   Finish by placing a strip of milk chocolate on the coffee éclairs and a strip of dark chocolate on the chocolate éclairs.

NOTES: When you make the choux pastry, you can add the eggs all at once, instead of in thirds, as many recipes call for.

When making the chocolate pastry cream, be sure that the pastry cream and the cooled chocolate are the same temperature, so they emulsify well.

Florentine Tartlets

ACTIVE TIME	RESTING TIME	COOKING TIME
30 minutes	*1 hour*	*1 hour 30 minutes*

In recent years, it has become increasingly common in France to find cakes made with walnuts, almonds, hazelnuts, and pecans. This trend led me to consider their culinary potential.

While at first glance this tart might seem quite ordinary, its originality lies in the subtle addition of orange zest, which enhances the nuts' flavors. While sweet shortcrust pastry is used in traditional Florentine tarts, I feel a flaky puff-pastry crust is more suited to nuts.

Makes 6

EQUIPMENT

1	*4 ⅓-inch (11-cm) round pastry cutter*
6	*3-inch (8-cm) tart rings*
1	*instant-read thermometer*

—

TART SHELLS

480 G	*inverse puff pastry* (P. 172)

—

NUTS AND RAISINS

60 G	*walnuts*
60 G	*pecans*
30 G	*whole hazelnuts, skin on*
11 G	*whole shelled pistachios*
45 G	*raisins*

—

FLORENTINE CARAMEL

75 G	*heavy cream*
45 G	*wildflower honey* (SEE NOTES)
75 G	*demerara sugar*
75 G	*unsalted butter*
	finely grated zest of ¼ orange

—

DECORATION

*snow sugar
(non-melting sugar)*

Tart shells

01.   On a work surface, roll out the puff pastry to a thickness of 2 mm. Cut out 6 disks of dough using the pastry cutter. Line a baking sheet with parchment paper and place the tart rings on the sheet. Lay the dough over the tart rings and gently tuck it into the corners and against the sides, letting the excess dough hang over the rim. Place in the refrigerator for 1 hour.

02.   Preheat the oven to 340°F (170 °C). Prick the dough with a fork. Line each tart shell with parchment paper and top with pie weights. Bake for 25 to 30 minutes.

Nuts and raisins

01.   Preheat the oven to 315 °F (155°C). Spread the walnuts and pecans on a baking sheet lined with parchment paper. Toast them in the oven for 25 minutes until they are golden brown. Set aside to cool.

02.   On separate baking sheets lined with parchment paper, toast the hazelnuts for 30–35 minutes and the pistachios for 15 minutes. Let cool completely, then rub the nuts together between your hands to remove the skins. Ensure that the raisins are not stuck together.

Florentine caramel

01.   Combine the heavy cream, honey, sugar, and butter in a saucepan, and heat, stirring, to 230°F (110 °C). Remove from heat and add the orange zest. Add the toasted nuts and raisins. Stir gently to keep the nuts whole.

Assembly and decoration

01.   Preheat the oven to 320°F (160 °C).

02.   Fill the prebaked pie crusts with 65 g of filling, ensuring that the nuts and caramel are evenly distributed in each tart. Bake for 16 minutes.

03.   Remove from the oven and let cool at room temperature. Lightly dust the edges of the tarts with snow sugar.

NOTES: Choose honey with a mild scent to keep the flavors balanced.

Also, monitor the tarts while they bake: overcooking will harden the caramel. If you want to avoid breaking a tooth, scrupulously respect the temperature and cooking times so the Florentine caramel remains soft.

4 P.M.

Chocolate Tart

ACTIVE TIME	RESTING TIME	COOKING TIME
45 minutes	*3 hours 30 minutes*	*40 minutes*

*Of all the ingredients available to pâtissiers, chocolate is, for many, in a league of its own.
This tart was created so that all the ingredients exalt the taste of chocolate.*

*The texture of the thin, chocolate-flavored sweet shortcrust pastry, and two kinds of ganache
and praline paste, create levels of flavors on the palate. The layers are simple, but the structure
of the aromas and flavors is the result of long reflection.*

Serves 4

EQUIPMENT

1	*10 ½ × 3 × ¾-inch (27 × 8 × 2-cm) oval tart ring*
1	*guitar sheet*
2	*pastry bags*
1	*⅛-inch (4-mm) plain tip*

—

DECORATIVE CHOCOLATE LAYER

100 G	*Valrhona Andoa Noire dark chocolate, 70% cacao*

—

TART SHELL

105 G	*chocolate sweet shortcrust pastry (P. 176)*
10 G	*hazelnut praline paste*

—

NOUGATINE HAZELNUTS

150 G	*whole shelled hazelnuts*
1 G	*pectin NH*
65 G	*superfine sugar, divided*
50 G	*unsalted butter*
23 G	*glucose syrup*
17 G	*heavy cream*

—

DARK CHOCOLATE GANACHE

35 G	*Valrhona Guanaja dark chocolate, 70% cacao, chopped*
35 G	*Valrhona Andoa Noire dark chocolate, 70% cacao, chopped*
85 G	*heavy cream*

—

MILK CHOCOLATE GANACHE

25 G	*Valrhona Jivara milk chocolate, 40% cacao, chopped*
35 G	*heavy cream*

—

DECORATION

	unsweetened cocoa powder

Decorative chocolate layer

01.   Temper the chocolate (see Tempering Chocolate, pp. 180-181). Spread the tempered chocolate into a thin layer over one of the guitar sheets. Let the chocolate set briefly until it is firm but not yet hard, then use the tart ring to cut out a circle of chocolate.

Tart shell

01.   On a lightly floured surface, roll the pastry until it is ⅒ inch (3 mm) wider than the tart ring. Line the ring with the dough: lay the dough over the ring and gently press it into the corners and against the sides.

Nougatine hazelnuts

01.   Preheat the oven to 325°F (160°C). Spread the hazelnuts across a baking sheet lined with parchment paper and toast them in the oven for 25 to 30 minutes, until they are deeply golden. Remove and set aside to cool. Increase the oven temperature to 340°F (170°C).

02.   Combine the pectin and 10 g of the superfine sugar in a small bowl. Combine the remaining 55 g of superfine sugar with the butter and glucose in a large heavy saucepan and bring to a boil. Whisk in the cream. Reduce the heat to low, whisk in the pectin and sugar, and cook over low heat, whisking continuously for 30 seconds, or until the mixture starts to caramelize slightly. Turn off the heat and stir in the toasted hazelnuts.

03.   Immediately pour the hazelnut nougatine mixture onto a baking sheet lined with parchment paper and bake at 340°F (170°C) for 20 minutes, until the edges are golden. Remove the baking sheet from the oven and toss the nuts so those on the edges move to the center of the sheet. Return to the oven for 5 to 7 minutes to finish caramelizing.

04.   Remove the sheet from the oven. While the nuts are still warm, and wearing plastic gloves over oven mitts, roll the hazelnuts one by one to ensure that the nougatine is evenly distributed. Let cool at room temperature.

Dark chocolate ganache

01.   Place the dark chocolate in a medium bowl. In a medium saucepan, bring the cream to a boil. Remove from the heat, add half the cream to the dark chocolate, and whisk until melted and smooth. Add the rest of the cream and whisk until smooth. Transfer to a pastry bag fitted with the ⅛-inch (4-mm) plain tip.

Milk chocolate ganache

01.   Place the milk chocolate in a medium bowl. In a medium saucepan, bring the cream to a boil. Remove from the heat, add half the cream to the milk chocolate, and whisk until melted and smooth. Add half of the remaining cream, whisk well, then add the rest of the cream and whisk until smooth.

Assembly and decoration

01.   Fill the other pastry bag with the hazelnut praline paste and pipe it onto the bottom of the crust. Then pipe the shell three-quarters full with chocolate ganache. Let rest in the refrigerator for 30 minutes.

02.   Using a spoon, transfer the milk chocolate ganache to the tart shell. Let rest in the refrigerator for 2 hours until set and firm.

03.   Line the edge of the tart with nougatine hazelnuts. Dust the decorative chocolate layer with cocoa powder, then place it on top of the tart.

NOTES: Baking the chocolate shortcrust pastry at a low temperature ensures the flour is well-cooked, eliminates humidity, and makes for a flaky crust.

Keep the tart in the refrigerator and take it out 15 minutes before serving.

1
3
2

Brownies

ACTIVE TIME
30 minutes

COOKING TIME
40 minutes

First created in Chicago, this treat now has fans all over the world. It may be an everyday confection, but a pastry chef's mission is to celebrate ordinary desserts as much as fancy ones, and I never put one above the other. This recipe is not about originality—just pure pleasure.

However, I did make a few improvements to accommodate the French palate, which is more familiar with the real taste of chocolate. I recommend chocolate with a high cacao percentage (61% as opposed to the 50% called for in classic recipes). This is how I imagine brownies.

Serves 10

EQUIPMENT

1	*instant-read thermometer*
1	*9 × 9 × 1-inch (22.5 × 22.5 × 3.5-cm) pastry frame or cake pan*

—

BROWNIE BATTER

100 G	*walnuts*
100 G	*pecans*
220 G	*unsalted butter, at room temperature*
300 G	*granulated sugar*
2 G	*fine sea salt*
½	*vanilla bean, split lengthwise*
240 G	*beaten eggs (about 5 large eggs)*
80 G	*all-purpose flour (T45)*
170 G	*Valrhona Extra Bitter dark chocolate, 61% cacao, chopped*

—

DECORATION

whole walnuts
whole pecans

Brownie batter

01.   Preheat the oven to 340°F (170°C). Spread the walnuts and pecans across a baking sheet lined with parchment paper and toast for 10 minutes.

02.   In a bowl, mix together the butter, sugar, and salt. Scrape the vanilla bean seeds into the bowl.

03.   Heat the eggs in a small bowl set over a saucepan of barely simmering water until they reach (86°F) 30°C.

04.   Add one-quarter of the eggs to the butter mixture. Combine well. Repeat three more times with the remaining eggs. Add the flour and mix until well blended.

05.   Melt the chocolate in the microwave until it reaches 100°F (38°C). Pour it over the butter and egg mixture and mix until well blended. Stir in the toasted walnuts and pecans.

06.   Line the interior of the baking frame with parchment paper, and place it on a baking sheet. Line the interior with parchment paper. Pour the batter into the pan and distribute evenly using an offset spatula.

Baking

01.   Arrange the walnuts and pecans on top of the batter. Bake for 40 minutes.

02.   Remove from the oven and let cool 10 minutes before removing the frame. Let the brownies cool completely. Remove the parchment paper just before serving.

NOTE : The key to success is to ensure that the temperature is maintained during preparation 100°F (38°C) and to choose a good quality chocolate. There is no mystery!

Cocoa Macarons

ACTIVE TIME	RESTING TIME	CUISSON
30 minutes	*3 hours*	*26 minutes*

In my view, cocoa has infinite potential as an ingredient, so it was a natural choice for this creation. According to a Japanese proverb, it's when you love something that you can improve on it.

So, to highlight the flavor of cocoa—particularly by using less sugar—I created a macaron recipe using French meringue. Today, most macarons call for Italian meringue, which simplifies the process of making large quantities, but I decided to prioritize the flavor of the chocolate.

Makes 20 macarons

EQUIPMENT

1	*stand mixer*
2	*pastry bags*
1	*½-inch (12-mm) plain tip*
1	*1 ½-inch (3.5-cm) round pastry cutter*

—

MACARON SHELLS

175 G	*confectioners' sugar*
90 G	*almond flour*
9 G	*unsweetened cocoa powder*
110 G	*egg whites (about 4 whites from large eggs)*
23 G	*superfine sugar*
	cocoa nibs

—

DARK CHOCOLATE GANACHE

50 G	*Valrhona Guanaja dark chocolate, 70% cacao, chopped*
50 G	*Valrhona Andoa Noire dark chocolate, 70% cacao, chopped*
95 G	*heavy cream*
35 G	*unsalted butter, at room temperature*

Macaron shells

01.   Prepare a French meringue. Sift together the confectioners' sugar, almond flour, and cocoa powder. In the bowl of a stand mixer fitted with the whisk attachment, beat the egg whites and sugar on high speed. When stiff peaks begin to form, add the dry ingredients, and fold in with a flexible spatula using the macaronnage technique: with a circular motion, cutting down through the top, toward you, and then back over again toward the center of the bowl, until the batter is shiny. Transfer to a pastry bag fitted with the plain tip.

02.   Using the pastry cutter, draw twenty 1 ¼-inch (3.5-cm) circles on a sheet of parchment paper as a template for piping the macaron shells. Turn the paper over, place it on a baking sheet, and pipe out meringue to fill the circles. Gently tap the baking sheet against a work surface to distribute the meringue more evenly. Arrange about five cocoa nibs on each shell and dust with cocoa powder using a fine-mesh sieve. Let dry at room temperature for about 3 hours.

03.   Preheat the oven to 300°F (150°C). Bake the macaron shells at this temperature for 4 minutes, then open the oven door slightly, lower the temperature to 250°F (120°C), and bake for 2 minutes. Close the oven door and continue to bake for 15 to 20 minutes, until the shells can be easily lifted off the parchment paper. Remove from the oven and let cool completely on the baking sheet.

Dark chocolate ganache

01.   Place both chocolates in a large bowl. In a saucepan, bring the cream to a boil. Remove from the heat, pour half the cream over the chocolate, and whisk until melted and smooth. When the chocolate has melted, add the rest of the cream. When the mixture is smooth, add the softened butter and mix well. Transfer the ganache to a bowl and cover with plastic wrap. Let rest in the refrigerator for 30 minutes.

Assembly

01.   Using your thumb, make a slight indentation in the center of each shell. Fill the other pastry bag with the ganache and pipe 8 g of ganache over half of the shells: position the tip in the center of the shell, applying pressure as you pipe to form a small dome that covers the entire surface of the shell. Top with a second macaron shell. Repeat with the remaining shells.

NOTES: For successful macarons, beat the meringue until it holds stiff peaks. Using the spatula, draw the batter about 12 inches (30 cm) above the bowl. If it forms a ribbon, it is ready. If not, continue the macaronnage.

2 Place Saint-Michel, Paris 6th Arrondissement – 8:05 p.m.

CHAP. 6

Evening

Mont Blanc

ACTIVE TIME
1 hour

COOKING TIME
15 minutes

It goes without saying that the chestnut flavor is king here. The shape of this Mont Blanc was chosen not to give the pastry an "iconic" look but rather for the sake of taste. When considering the balance between the chestnut cream and the phyllo pastry, the obvious choice was to use more cream, hence the mountain of it in the center. Here, form follows flavor.

Yet the texture of the phyllo pastry is of utmost importance, as it remains crisp into the evening— unlike other pastry crusts that absorb moisture quickly and must be eaten right away.

Serves 4 to 5

EQUIPMENT

1	*6-inch (15-cm) tart ring*
3	*pastry bags*
1	*½-inch (12-mm) plain tip*
1	*stand mixer*
1	*⅔-inch (16-mm) star tip (PF16)*
1	*Mont Blanc tip*

—

MONT BLANC BASE

60 G	*melted unsalted butter + more as needed*
3	*sheets phyllo dough* (SEE NOTES)
130 G	*almond cream* (P. 177)

—

WHIPPED CREAM

155 G	*heavy cream, cold*
30 G	*mascarpone, cold*
15 G	*superfine sugar*

—

CHESTNUT CREAM

70 G	*chestnut paste (pâte de marrons)*
145 G	*chestnut purée (purée de marrons)*
8 G	*dark rum*
50 G	*pastry cream* (P. 170)
25 G	*whipped cream* (SEE ABOVE)

—

ASSEMBLY

10	*candied chestnuts snow sugar (non-melting sugar)*

Mont Blanc base

01.   Preheat the oven to 340°F (170°C). Brush a thin layer of melted butter over one sheet of phyllo dough. Cover with a second sheet and brush with butter. Repeat for the third and final layer.

02.   Cut the dough into an 8-inch (20-cm) square and line the tart ring with it (see Lining a Tart Ring with Phyllo Dough, p. 178).

03.   Fit one of the pastry bags with the ½-inch (12-mm) plain tip and fill it with the almond cream. Pipe the almond cream onto the tart base in a spiral, starting in the center and working your way outward to the edge. Bake for 15 minutes, until golden and crisp, then let cool completely.

Whipped cream

01.   Fit the stand mixer with the whisk attachment and place the cream, mascarpone, and sugar in the bowl. Beat on high speed until stiff peaks form.

02.   Weigh out 25 g of the whipped cream and set aside for making the chestnut cream. Transfer the remaining whipped cream to a pastry bag fitted with the ⅔-inch (16-mm) star tip and reserve in the refrigerator.

Chestnut cream

01.   Combine the chestnut paste and chestnut purée in a medium bowl, then stir in the rum until well blended. Using a bowl scraper, press the mixture through a fine-mesh sieve into a large bowl.

02.   Fold the pastry cream into the chestnut mixture, then gently fold in the 25 g reserved whipped cream. Transfer the chestnut cream to the third pastry bag fitted with the Mont Blanc tip.

Assembly

SEE THE STEP-BY-STEP INSTRUCTIONS ON PAGE 143.

→

NOTES: Using phyllo pastry instead of the traditional meringue was a logical solution to me, as the latter quickly loses its crisp texture and also makes the whole cake too sweet. I use several layers of phyllo dough to accentuate the contrast between the base and the filling. Phyllo dough can dry out quickly, however, so don't open the package until the last minute.

Step-by-Step

ASSEMBLING THE MONT BLANC

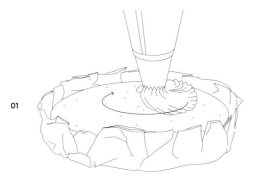

01

Pipe a layer of whipped cream over the phyllo base.

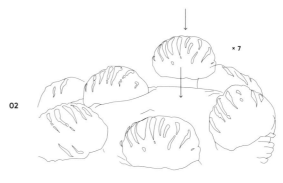

02

× 7

Arrange the whole candied chestnuts over the top.

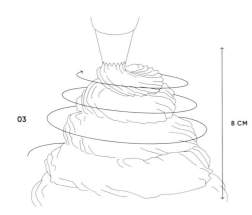

03

8 CM

⅔-INCH (16-MM)
STAR TIP (PF16)

Pipe a 3-inch (8-cm)-high dome of
whipped cream in the center.

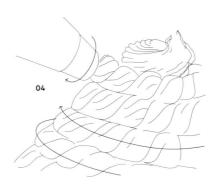

04

MONT-BLANC
TIP

Pipe swirls of chestnut-cream strings over
the whipped cream dome by making small
circular movements with your hand, starting
at the base and working your way up.

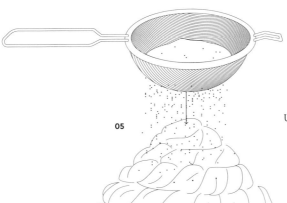

05

Using a fine-mesh sieve, dust evenly
with snow sugar.

Beige

ACTIVE TIME	RESTING TIME	COOKING TIME
1 hour	*3 hours*	*20 minutes*

This dessert originated as a chocolate mousse cake called "Noir."
But I modified the recipe one early spring when the weather began to turn warm.
I wanted something that could replace the chocolate, a winter ingredient, yet still maintain
the texture-flavor equilibrium.

With its light, delicate taste, tea was a perfect fit.
After experimenting with different types of tea, I fell for Earl Grey with its bergamot notes.
Regulars kept asking me for this spring version, so I added it to my year-round repertoire.

Serves 6

EQUIPMENT

1	*10-inch (25-cm) round pastry cutter*
1	*8-inch (20-cm) tart ring, ¾ inch (2 cm) deep*
1	*7½-inch (19-cm) tart ring, ¾ inch (2 cm) deep*
1	*instant-read thermometer*
1	*guitar sheet*
1	*chocolate spray gun or toothbrush*

—

WHITE CHOCOLATE PETALS

300 G	*white chocolate*
30 G	*sunflower oil*

—

CHOCOLATE TART SHELL

200 G	*chocolate sweet shortcrust pastry* (P. 176)

—

FEUILLETINE LAYER

55 G	*almond praline paste*
15 G	*Valrhona Extra Bitter dark chocolate, 61% cacao, chopped*
20 G	*Valrhona Jivara milk chocolate, 40% cacao, chopped*
	finely grated zest of ½ lime
55 G	*feuilletine flakes*

—

LIGHT GANACHE

150 G	*heavy cream*
	finely grated zest of ½ orange
20 G	*Valrhona Extra Bitter dark chocolate, 61% cacao, chopped*
80 G	*Valrhona Jivara milk chocolate, 40% cacao, chopped*

White chocolate petals

01.   Temper the white chocolate together with the sunflower oil using your method of choice (see Tempering Chocolate, pp. 180–181). While the tempered chocolate is still warm, pour it into a baking dish and let it set before assembling the cake.

Chocolate tart shell

01.   Preheat the oven to 330°F (165°C). On a lightly floured surface, roll the pastry to a thickness of ⅟₁₆ inch (2 mm). Cut out a 10-inch (25-cm) disk using the pastry cutter. Place the 8-inch (20-cm) tart ring on a baking sheet lined with parchment paper and line the ring with the dough: lay the dough over the ring and gently press it into the corners and against the sides. Trim the edges using a sharp knife. Place the baking sheet in the refrigerator for 10 minutes.

02.   Bake the pastry for 20 minutes, until fully set. Let it cool completely, then remove the tart ring.

Feuilletine layer

01.   Place the praline paste and both chocolates in a small bowl set over a saucepan of barely simmering water. Cook, stirring, until the mixture has melted and reached about 104°F (40°C). Remove the bowl from the saucepan and stir in the lime zest and feuilletine flakes. While the mixture is still hot, pour 140 g into the tart shell and spread it into an even layer using the back of a spoon.

Light ganache

01.   Combine the cream and orange zest in a large saucepan and bring to a boil. Remove from the heat, add both chocolates, and whisk until melted and smooth.

02.   Transfer the ganache to a bowl and let it cool completely, then pour it over the feuilletine layer in the tart shell and place in the refrigerator until set.

→

"Each time I arrange my pastries in the display case, I imagine what sensations they might give my customers, what emotions they might evoke. In what situations or on what occasions will they be eaten? I hope they'll be a source of joy and delight."

EARL GREY MOUSSE

6 G	*gelatin powder*
30 G	*water, heated to 122°F (50°C)*
195 G	*whole milk*
230 G	*heavy cream*
	finely grated zest of ½ lime
7 G	*loose-leaf Earl Grey tea*
80 G	*egg yolks (about 4 yolks from large eggs)*
60 G	*granulated sugar*
90 G	*heavy cream, whipped to stiff peaks*

—

WHITE VELVET COATING

50 G	*cocoa butter*
100 G	*white chocolate*

—

DECORATION

loose-leaf Earl Grey tea
finely grated lime zest
cornflower petals

Earl Grey mousse

01.   In a small bowl, dissolve the gelatin powder in the 122°F (50°C) water. Combine the milk, cream, and lime zest in a medium saucepan and bring to a boil. Remove from the heat, stir in the tea leaves, and cover. Let steep for 5 minutes, then remove the lid, stir gently, and strain through a fine-mesh sieve into a clean large saucepan.

02.   Warm the tea-steeped milk mixture to just before a boil, then remove the saucepan from the heat. In a medium bowl, whisk together the egg yolks and sugar. Whisking continuously, gradually pour one-third of the hot milk mixture into the egg yolk mixture, then pour everything back into the saucepan. Stirring nonstop with a flexible spatula, cook until the custard reaches 172°F (78°C), then remove it from the heat and stir in the dissolved gelatin. Strain the custard through a fine-mesh sieve into a bowl and set it over a larger bowl filled with ice water to cool it quickly. Leave the bowl over ice water, stirring often, until the custard thickens and reaches 41°F (5°C). Fold in the whipped cream.

03.   Place the 7½-inch (19-cm) tart ring on a baking sheet lined with the guitar sheet. Pour the Earl Grey mousse into the ring and freeze for at least 3 hours or until thoroughly frozen.

04.   When the mousse is thoroughly frozen, warm the ring slightly with your hands and remove it. Return the mousse layer to the freezer until applying the white velvet coating.

White velvet coating and assembly

01.   Place the cocoa butter and white chocolate together in a medium bowl set over a saucepan of barely simmering water. Cook, stirring, until the mixture has melted and reached about 104°F (40°C). Transfer to the chocolate spray gun if you are using one. Remove the Earl Grey mousse layer from the freezer and immediately spray it evenly with the white velvet mixture. Alternatively, you can apply the velvet coating using a toothbrush: dip the toothbrush into the mixture and run your thumb along the bristles to spray the surface of the mousse.

02.   Remove the tart base from the refrigerator and set the velvet-coated mousse layer over the firm ganache. Let thaw before serving.

Decoration

01. Right before serving, scrape the tempered and set white chocolate using a spoon to obtain 10 petals and arrange over half of the gâteau. Sprinkle the other half with Earl Grey tea leaves, lime zest, and cornflower petals.

M

ACTIVE TIME	RESTING TIME	COOKING TIME
1 hour	*8 hours*	*45 minutes*

I created this gâteau to combine a range of toasted flavors, from nuts and cacao beans to sugar transformed into caramel. The caramel in this recipe is made with maple sugar, which contains minerals such as potassium, magnesium, and calcium. This makes it tricky to caramelize, but it produces a more complex taste than regular sugar.

Serves 6

EQUIPMENT

3	*12 × 8-inch (30 × 20-cm) guitar sheets*
1	*22 × 14-inch (56 × 36-cm) pastry frame*
1	*instant-read thermometer*
1	*stand mixer + 2 mixer bowls*
1	*refractometer (optional)*
1	*pastry bag*
1	*triangular bûche (Yule log) mold, 12 × 3 × 2 inches (30 × 8 cm × 5.5 cm)*

———

CHOCOLATE TRIANGLES

300 G	*Valrhona Guanaja dark chocolate, 70% cacao, tempered and still warm* (PP. 180–181)
	maple sugar

———

MANDARIN CONFIT

50 G	*peeled mandarin (about 1 small mandarin)*
45 G	*granulated sugar*

———

HAZELNUT JOCONDE SPONGE

280 G	*lightly beaten eggs (about 5½ large eggs), at room temperature*
275 G	*egg whites (about 9 whites from large eggs), at room temperature, divided*
145 G	*almond flour*
230 G	*hazelnut flour*
230 G	*confectioners' sugar*
185 G	*unsalted butter*
70 G	*pastry flour (T45)*
85 G	*superfine sugar*

———

NOUGATINE HAZELNUTS

170 G	*whole hazelnuts*
1.5 G	*pectin NH*
80 G	*superfine sugar, divided*
55 G	*unsalted butter*
25 G	*glucose syrup*
20 G	*heavy cream*

Chocolate triangles

01. Spread the tempered chocolate into a thin layer over one of the guitar sheets and sprinkle it with maple sugar before it sets. Let the chocolate set briefly until it is firm but not yet hard, then cut isosceles triangles using the tip of a sharp knife—they should be 2 inches (5 cm) at the base and 8 inches (20 cm) high. With the chocolate side facing down, roll the sheet around a rolling pin or cylinder with a diameter of at least 1½ inches (4 cm). Let the triangles set, then peel them off the guitar sheet.

Mandarin confit

01. Separate the mandarin into segments and cut each segment into ¼-inch (5-mm) pieces. Place the pieces in a small saucepan with the sugar and mix carefully to distribute the sugar evenly without crushing the fruit. Let macerate at room temperature for 2 hours.

02. Bring the mandarin-sugar mixture to a boil. If you have a refractometer, use it to check the sugar content. Continue to cook until the mixture reaches 40° to 45° Brix. If you do not have a refractometer, let the mixture cook at a boil for 2 to 3 minutes. Transfer to a bowl, press plastic wrap over the surface, and let cool in the refrigerator.

03. Once the confit has cooled completely, transfer it to the pastry bag. Line the bûche mold with one of the guitar sheets and pipe 20 g of the confit down the center.

Hazelnut Joconde sponge

01. Preheat the oven to 340°F (170°C) and place the pastry frame on a baking sheet lined with parchment paper. Whisk together the eggs and 125 g of the egg whites (about 4 whites) in a large bowl set over a saucepan of barely simmering water. Whisking, heat the eggs to about 104°F (40°C). Transfer to one of the stand mixer bowls and fit the mixer with the whisk attachment. Sift in the almond flour, hazelnut flour, and confectioners' sugar together, then beat on high speed until the mixture is pale and thick.

02. Melt the butter to 122°F (50°C) in a large bowl set over a saucepan of barely simmering water. Remove from the heat and whisk in one-fourth of the beaten egg mixture until emulsified. Sift the pastry flour into the mixer bowl with the rest of the egg mixture and gently fold it in.

03. Combine the remaining 150 g egg whites with the superfine sugar in the second mixer bowl and beat until the whites hold firm peaks.

04. Using a flexible spatula, gently fold the whites into the egg and flour mixture until only a few white streaks remain, then fold in the butter mixture until well blended.

05. Pour the batter into the pastry frame and smooth it into an even layer using an offset spatula. Bake for 20 minutes.

06. Gently slide a spatula between the frame and the sponge to remove the frame. Then, carefully transfer the sponge to a rack and let it cool.

07. Once the sponge has cooled completely, cut out a 12 × 3-inch (30 × 8-cm) rectangle.

Nougatine hazelnuts

01. Preheat the oven to 325°F (160°C). Spread the hazelnuts across a baking sheet lined with parchment paper and toast them in the oven for 25 to 30 minutes, until they are deeply golden. Remove and set aside to cool. Increase the oven temperature to 340°F (170°C).

02. Combine the pectin and 15 g of the superfine sugar in a small bowl. Combine the remaining 65 g of superfine sugar with the butter and glucose in a large heavy saucepan and bring to a boil. Whisk in the cream. Reduce the heat to low, whisk in the pectin and sugar, and cook over low heat, whisking continuously for 30 seconds, or until the mixture starts to caramelize slightly. Turn off the heat and stir in the toasted hazelnuts.

03. Immediately pour the hazelnut nougatine mixture onto a baking sheet lined with parchment paper and bake at 340°F (170°C) for 20 minutes, until the edges are golden. Remove the baking sheet from the oven and toss the nuts so those on the edges move to the center of the sheet. Return to the oven for 5 to 7 minutes to finish caramelizing. Let cool, then chop roughly.

→

CARAMELIZED MAPLE CREAM

4.5 G *gelatin powder*

22 G *water, heated to 122°F (50°C)*

215 G *heavy cream*

65 G *maple sugar*

70 G *egg yolks (about 3½ yolks from large eggs)*

25 G *demerara sugar*

80 G *heavy cream, whipped to stiff peaks*

—

CHOCOLATE-MAPLE MOUSSE

95 G *heavy cream*

45 G *maple sugar*

120 G *Valrhona Guanaja dark chocolate, 70% cacao, chopped*

40 G *egg yolks (2 yolks from large eggs)*

25 G *demerara sugar*

225 G *heavy cream, whipped to soft peaks*

—

CHOCOLATE-HAZELNUT GLAZE

6 G *gelatin powder*

30 G *water, heated to 122°F (50°C)*

20 G *hazelnut praline paste*

75 G *Valrhona Extra Bitter dark chocolate, 61% cacao, chopped*

200 G *heavy cream*

30 G *invert sugar (Trimoline®)*

25 G *superfine sugar*

10 G *unsweetened cocoa powder*

—

DECORATION

nougatine hazelnuts
unsweetened cocoa powder

Caramelized maple cream

01. In a small bowl, dissolve the gelatin powder in the 122°F (50°C) water. In a small saucepan, warm the cream over medium heat until just before it comes to a boil, then remove from the heat. In a large dry saucepan, melt the maple sugar over low heat, stirring continuously (see notes). Still stirring, pour in the hot cream to stop the caramel from cooking further. If some of the sugar recrystallizes, keep stirring over low heat until it melts again (see notes). Bring the mixture to a boil.

02. In a medium bowl, whisk together the egg yolks and demerara sugar. Whisking continuously, gradually pour one-third of the hot cream mixture into the egg yolk mixture. Pour back into the saucepan, whisking continuously. Still whisking, cook over medium heat until the custard thickens and reaches 172°F (78°C). Remove from heat and stir in the dissolved gelatin.

03. Strain the custard through a fine-mesh sieve into a bowl and set it over a larger bowl filled with ice water to cool it quickly. Leave the bowl over the ice water, stirring often, until the custard thickens and reaches 41°F (5°C). Fold in the whipped cream.

04. Ladle 300 g of the caramelized maple cream over the mandarin confit in the bûche mold. Gently tilt the mold from right to left to distribute the cream evenly. Freeze for about 3 hours, or until thoroughly frozen. Turn out of the mold and return to the freezer—you can leave it in the guitar sheet.

Chocolate-maple mousse

01. In a small saucepan, warm the cream over medium heat until just before it comes to a boil, then remove from the heat. In a large dry saucepan, melt the maple sugar over low heat, stirring continuously (see notes). Still stirring, pour in the hot cream to stop the caramel from cooking further. If some of the sugar recrystallizes, keep stirring over low heat until it melts again (see notes). Bring the mixture to a boil.

02. Place the chocolate in a large bowl. In a separate medium bowl, whisk together the egg yolks and demerara sugar. Whisking continuously, gradually pour one-third of the hot cream mixture into the egg yolk mixture. Pour back into the saucepan, whisking continuously. Still whisking, cook over medium heat until the custard thickens and reaches 172°F (78°C). Remove from the heat and strain through a fine-mesh sieve into the bowl with the chocolate. Whisk until smooth, then fold in the whipped cream.

03. Line the bûche mold with a clean guitar sheet. Using a ladle, pour 350 g of the chocolate-maple mousse into the mold. Remove the maple cream and mandarin confit layer from the freezer and nestle it into the mousse, then add a little more mousse on top and smooth it into an even layer. Scatter roughly chopped nougatine hazelnuts over the mousse, reserving some for decoration. Cover with the hazelnut Joconde biscuit rectangle and press down firmly to ensure that the sponge sticks to the mousse. Freeze for 3 hours, or until thoroughly frozen.

Chocolate-hazelnut glaze

01. In a small bowl, dissolve the gelatin powder in the 122°F (50°C) water. Place the hazelnut praline paste and chocolate in a large bowl. Combine the cream and invert sugar in a large saucepan and bring to a boil. In a separate small bowl, combine the superfine sugar and cocoa powder. Stir one-fourth of the sugar-cocoa mixture into the saucepan, then stir in the remaining three-fourths. Stir in the dissolved gelatin until well blended.

02. Pour one-third of this hot mixture over the praline paste and chocolate and whisk until smooth. Add the rest and mix until well blended. Pass the glaze through a fine-mesh sieve into a clean bowl, press plastic wrap over the surface, and let cool to about 82°F (28°C).

Assembly and decoration

01. Remove the frozen component from the freezer, turn it out of the mold, and peel off the guitar sheet. Trim 2 inches (5 cm) off each end and place on a rack. Pour the glaze over it until it is well-coated and let it sit for 30 seconds, then carefully transfer it to a serving plate. Top with 5 chocolate triangles, attempting to form a spiral.

02. Arrange pieces of hazelnut nougatine in a diagonal line running from one side of the gâteau to the other. Using a fine-mesh sieve, dust cocoa powder over one-third of the top, starting from the undecorated edge.

NOTES: Maple sugar is not as easy to work with as cane or beet sugar. To caramelize it, place it in a dry heavy saucepan and melt it over low heat, stirring continuously to blend the melted sugar with the not-yet-melted parts. Make sure the sugar does not burn on the bottom of the pan. If you notice it is starting to burn, remove the saucepan from the heat and stir well, then return it to low heat until all the sugar has melted. When you add the cream to stop the cooking, some of the sugar may recrystallize and form lumps, so keep stirring over low heat until it melts again and is integrated into the cream.

Getting the timing of the caramelization right is the hardest part of this recipe. Even in our boutique, I'm still the only one on the team who makes this gâteau.

Vanillier

ACTIVE TIME
1 hour

RESTING TIME
5 hours

COOKING TIME
20 minutes

Vanilla reigns in this gâteau, which I created to thoroughly explore all the nuances of this magnificent plant, which opened the doors for me to a deep world of aromas and flavors. I've always loved the taste of Tahitian vanilla, but after several experiments, I concluded that Madagascar vanilla pairs best with dairy.

The grainy texture of the base is fundamental, as it produces a sensation that "reaches" the brain, if I dare say so. Without texture, the sensation does not extend beyond our tongues. Texture alerts our brains, making the tasting experience more complex.

Makes 6

EQUIPMENT

1	*22 × 14-inch (56 × 36-cm) pastry frame*
1	*instant-read thermometer*
1	*stand mixer*
1	*2½-inch (6.5-cm) round pastry cutter*
1	*silicone mold with cavities that are 1½ inches round and ¾ inch (2 cm) deep*
1	*silicone mold with cavities that are 2½ inches (6.5 cm) round and 1½ inches (4 cm) deep*

—

ALMOND JOCONDE SPONGE

280 G	*lightly beaten eggs (about 5½ large eggs), at room temperature*
275 G	*egg whites (about 9 whites from large eggs), at room temperature, divided*
375 G	*almond flour*
230 G	*confectioners' sugar*
185 G	*unsalted butter*
70 G	*pastry flour (T45)*
85 G	*superfine sugar*

—

FEUILLETINE LAYER

30 G	*almond praline paste*
15 G	*Valrhona Ivoire white chocolate, 35% cacao, chopped*
35 G	*feuilletine flakes*

—

VANILLA GANACHE

125 G	*heavy cream*
½	*Madagascar vanilla bean (SEE NOTES), split lengthwise*
1 G	*gelatin powder*
5 G	*water, heated to 122°F (50°C)*

Almond Joconde sponge

01. Preheat the oven to 340°F (170°C) and place the pastry frame on a baking sheet lined with parchment paper. Whisk together the eggs and 125 g of the egg whites (about 4 whites) in a large bowl set over a saucepan of barely simmering water. Whisking, heat the eggs to about 104°F (40°C). Transfer to one of the stand mixer bowls and fit the mixer with the whisk attachment. Sift the almond flour and confectioners' sugar into the bowl, then beat on high speed until the mixture is pale and thick.

02. Melt the butter to 122°F (50°C) in a large bowl set over a saucepan of barely simmering water. Remove from the heat and whisk in one-fourth of the beaten egg mixture until emulsified. Sift the pastry flour into the mixer bowl with the rest of the egg mixture and gently fold it in.

03. Combine the remaining 150 g egg whites with the superfine sugar in the second mixer bowl and beat with the whisk attachment until the whites hold stiff peaks.

04. Using a flexible spatula, gently fold the whites into the egg and flour mixture until only a few white streaks remain, then fold in the butter mixture until well blended.

05. Pour the batter into the pastry frame and smooth it into an even layer using an offset spatula. Bake for 20 minutes, until the cake is set and golden.

06. Gently slide a spatula between the frame and the sponge to remove the frame. Then, carefully transfer the sponge to a rack and let it cool.

07. Once the sponge has cooled completely, cut out six disks using the 2½-inch (6.5-cm) pastry cutter.

Feuilletine layer

01. Place the praline paste and chocolate in a small bowl set over a saucepan of barely simmering water. Cook, stirring, until the mixture has melted and reached about 104°F (40°C). Remove the bowl from the saucepan and stir in the feuilletine flakes. Spread a thin layer of the mixture (about ⅒ inch/3 mm) over the Joconde sponge disks. Place in the refrigerator for at least 10 minutes or until using.

Vanilla ganache

01. Pour the cream into a small saucepan, scrape in the vanilla bean seeds, and drop in the vanilla pod. Bring to a boil, then remove from the heat, cover, and let infuse for 30 minutes. Meanwhile, dissolve the gelatin powder in the 122°F (50°C) water in a small bowl and place the white chocolate in a large bowl. Bring the cream to a boil again, then strain it through a fine-mesh sieve into a small bowl (reserve the vanilla pod for decoration).

02. Pour one-third of the hot cream at a time over the chocolate and whisk until smooth after each addition. Mix in the dissolved gelatin. Place the mold with the 1½-inch (4-cm) cavities on a baking sheet and pour 5 g of vanilla ganache into each of six cavities. Place the baking sheet in the freezer to allow the ganache to harden.

→

VANILLA CREAM

40 G	*whole milk*
60 G	*heavy cream*
½	*Madagascar vanilla bean* (SEE NOTES), *split lengthwise*
20 G	*egg yolk (1 yolk from 1 large egg)*
20 G	*superfine sugar*
1.5 G	*gelatin powder*
8 G	*water, heated to 122°F (50°C)*

—

VANILLA MOUSSE

205 G	*heavy cream*
1	*Madagascar vanilla bean* (SEE NOTES), *split lengthwise*
4 G	*gelatin powder*
20 G	*water, heated to 122°F (50°C)*
40 G	*egg yolks (2 yolks from large eggs)*
54 G	*superfine sugar*
140 G	*heavy cream, whipped to stiff peaks, cold*
70 G	*mascarpone, cold*

—

VANILLA GLAZE

5 G	*gelatin powder*
25 G	*water, heated to 122°F (50°C)*
395 G	*Valrhona Ivoire white chocolate, 35% cacao, chopped*
180 G	*whole milk*
70 G	*glucose syrup*
1	*Madagascar vanilla bean* (SEE NOTES), *split lengthwise*

—

DECORATION

all the vanilla beans used in the recipe
superfine sugar

Vanilla cream

01. Combine the milk and cream in a small saucepan, scrape in the vanilla bean seeds, and drop in the vanilla pod. Bring to a boil, then remove from the heat, cover, and let infuse for 30 minutes. Meanwhile, in a small bowl, dissolve the gelatin powder in the 122°F (50°C) water.

02. In a medium bowl, whisk together the egg yolks and sugar. Return the infused cream mixture to a boil. Whisking continuously, gradually pour one-third of the hot cream mixture into the egg yolk mixture. Pour back into the saucepan, whisking continuously. Cook over medium heat, whisking, until the custard thickens and reaches 172°F (78°C).

03. Remove from heat and stir in the dissolved gelatin until well blended. Strain the custard through a fine-mesh sieve into a bowl (reserve the pod for decoration) and set over a larger bowl filled with ice water to cool it quickly. Leave the bowl over ice water, stirring often, until the custard thickens and reaches 41°F (5°C). Remove the mold with the vanilla ganache from the freezer and pour 15 g of vanilla cream over the ganache in each cavity. Freeze for 2 hours.

Vanilla mousse

01. Pour the cream into a medium saucepan and scrape in the vanilla bean seeds and drop in the vanilla pod. Bring to a boil, then remove from the heat, cover, and let infuse for 30 minutes. Meanwhile, in a small bowl, dissolve the gelatin powder in the 122°F (50°C) water.

02. In a medium bowl, whisk together the egg yolks and sugar. Whisking continuously, gradually pour one-third of the hot milk mixture into the egg yolk mixture, then pour everything back into the saucepan. Stirring nonstop, cook until the custard reaches 172°F (78°C).

03. Remove the saucepan from the heat and stir in the dissolved gelatin until well blended. Strain the custard through a fine-mesh sieve into a bowl (reserve the pod for decoration) and set it over a larger bowl filled with ice water to cool it quickly. Leave the bowl over ice water, stirring often, until the custard thickens and reaches 45°F (7°C).

04. Place the whipped cream and mascarpone in the bowl of the stand mixer fitted with the whisk attachment and beat together until the mixture holds stiff peaks. Fold into the cooled custard until well blended. Place the mold with the 2½-inch (6.5-cm) cavities on a baking sheet and spoon vanilla mousse into six of the cavities, filling them three-fourths full.

05. Remove the other mold from the freezer, turn out the layered vanilla cream and ganache disks, and nestle them into the vanilla mousse in the second mold. Cover with mousse. Run a spatula over the top to smooth it and remove any excess mousse, then place the Joconde sponge disks on top with the feuilletine layer facing down. Place in the freezer for at least 2 hours.

Vanilla glaze and decoration

01. In a small bowl, dissolve the gelatin powder in the 122°F (50°C) water. Place the chocolate in a large bowl. Combine the milk and glucose in a small saucepan, and scrape in the vanilla seeds and drop in the vanilla pod. Bring to a boil, then remove from the heat and stir in the dissolved gelatin. Pour one-third of the mixture at a time over the chocolate, whisking until smooth after each addition. Pass the glaze through a fine-mesh sieve into a clean bowl (reserve the pod for decoration). Press plastic wrap over the surface of the glaze and let it cool to 77°F (25°C).

02. When the glaze reaches 77°F (25°C), remove the mold from the freezer, turn out the frozen components, and place them on a rack. Pour the glaze over them, ensuring they are well coated.

03. Gather all the vanilla beans reserved from the recipe and cut the two whole beans crosswise in half. Wipe off excess liquid, then sprinkle them with superfine sugar.

04. Top each gâteau with a piece of sugar-coated vanilla bean. Refrigerate until serving (see notes).

NOTES: This recipe is designed to remain exceptionally soft and silky. Once it is prepared, store it in the refrigerator until you are ready to serve it.

For the best flavor, choose large vanilla beans, preferably between 6 and 8 inches (15–20 cm) long. Infusing the beans in cream and/or milk for at least 30 minutes helps distribute the flavor throughout the gâteau. When removing the beans from the liquid, squeeze out every last flavor-rich drop. This is where the flavor hides, and not in the seeds themselves.

Cannelés

ACTIVE TIME	RESTING TIME	COOKING TIME
30 minutes	*3 hours + 12 hours*	*1 hour 10 minutes*

Texture is obviously crucial in these cannelés, but the combination of vanilla, rum, and orange zest provides an equally important foundation. Traditional cannelés do not contain orange zest, but adding it lends an aroma and flavor that blossom in the mouth and linger on the finish.

To allow these three ingredients to shine, it is best to use relatively large molds rather than mini ones so that there is ample flavor packed inside each cannelé.

Makes 10 cannelés

EQUIPMENT

1	*instant-read thermometer*
10	*2-inch (5.5-cm) copper cannelé molds, 2 inches (5 cm) deep*

—

CANNELÉ BATTER

495 G	*whole milk*
50 G	*unsalted butter*
210 G	*superfine sugar*
3 G	*fine sea salt*
	Finely grated zest of ½ orange
1	*vanilla bean, split lengthwise*
60 G	*egg yolks (3 yolks from large eggs)*
25 G	*lightly beaten egg (about ½ large egg)*
100 G	*pastry flour (T45)*
20 G	*cornstarch*
50 G	*dark rum*

Cannelé batter

01.   The day before baking, combine the milk, butter, sugar, salt, and orange zest in a large saucepan. Scrape in the vanilla bean seeds and drop in the pod. Stirring continuously, heat the mixture to 176°F (80°C), then remove from the heat and let infuse for 3 hours.

02.   In a large bowl, whisk together the egg yolks and lightly beaten egg, then whisk in half of the infused milk mixture. Sift the flour and cornstarch together into the bowl and whisk until well combined. Whisk in the remaining infused milk mixture, followed by the rum.

03.   Pass the batter through a fine-mesh sieve into a clean bowl and let it rest overnight in the refrigerator. This allows any air trapped inside to escape and stabilizes the batter.

Baking

01.   The next day, preheat the oven to 340°F (170°C). Grease the molds with butter and place them on a baking sheet. Remove the batter from the refrigerator and, using a whisk, mix it well. Divide the batter between the molds, filling them just shy of the brim. Bake for 1 hour to 1 hour and 10 minutes, until the cannelés are a deep mahogany brown.

02.   Turn the cannelés out of the molds while they are still hot and place them on a rack to cool.

Souche de Noël

ACTIVE TIME	RESTING TIME	COOKING TIME
1 hour 30 minutes	*7 hours*	*20 minutes*

*Likely because I did not grow up in a Christian culture, each year, I ponder the meaning
of the bûche de Noël—especially because I lost my mother just as I was creating this gâteau.*

*I wanted to honor the deep, rich taste of chocolate and represent, in the form of a stump, my vision
of Christmas: life and death are not as far apart as we think, and new life can be born from a stump
we believe is dead. The spices are an homage to the traditional bûche recipe, as they were once used for their
medicinal properties and to preserve the cake. They also symbolize the essence, or soul, of the plants
they come from. Their aromas and flavors are the very energy of life itself.*

Serves 6 to 8

EQUIPMENT

1	*22 × 14-inch (56 × 36-cm) pastry frame*
1	*instant-read thermometer*
1	*stand mixer + 2 mixer bowls*
1	*6-inch (15-cm) tart ring, 1¼ inches (3 cm) deep*
1	*mortar and pestle*
1	*acetate (Rhodoïd) roll, 2½ inches (6 cm) wide*
2	*guitar sheets*
1	*refractometer (optional)*
2	*pastry bags*
1	*½-inch (12-mm) plain tip*
1	*7-inch (18-cm) baking ring, 2½ inches (6 cm) deep*
1	*chocolate spray gun (optional, see notes)*

—

HAZELNUT JOCONDE SPONGE

280 G	*lightly beaten eggs (about 5½ large eggs), at room temperature*
275 G	*egg whites (about 9 whites from large eggs), at room temperature, divided*
145 G	*almond flour*
230 G	*hazelnut flour*
230 G	*confectioners' sugar*
185 G	*unsalted butter*
70 G	*pastry flour (T45)*
85 G	*superfine sugar*

—

FEUILLETINE LAYER

30 G	*almond praline paste*
15 G	*Valrhona Ivoire white chocolate, 35% cacao, chopped*
35 G	*feuilletine flakes*

Hazelnut Joconde sponge

01. Preheat the oven to 340°F (170°C) and place the pastry frame on a baking sheet lined with parchment paper. Whisk together the eggs and 125 g of the egg whites (about 4 whites) in a large bowl set over a saucepan of barely simmering water. Whisking, heat the eggs to about 104°F (40°C). Transfer to one of the stand mixer bowls and fit the mixer with the whisk attachment. Sift in the almond flour, hazelnut flour, and confectioners' sugar together, then beat on high speed until the mixture is pale and thick.

02. Melt the butter to 122°F (50°C) in a large bowl set over a saucepan of barely simmering water. Remove from the heat and whisk in one-fourth of the beaten egg mixture until emulsified. Sift the pastry flour into the mixer bowl with the rest of the egg mixture and gently fold it in.

03. Combine the remaining 150 g egg whites with the superfine sugar in the second mixer bowl and beat until the whites hold stiff peaks.

04. Using a flexible spatula, gently fold the whites into the egg and flour mixture until only a few white streaks remain, then fold in the butter mixture until well blended.

05. Pour the batter into the pastry frame and smooth it into an even layer using an offset spatula. Bake for 20 minutes, until the cake is set and golden.

06. Gently slide a spatula between the frame and the sponge to remove the frame. Then, carefully transfer the sponge to a rack and let it cool.

07. Once the sponge has cooled completely, cut out a disk using the 6-inch (15-cm) tart ring.

Feuilletine layer

01. Place the praline paste and chocolate in a small bowl set over a saucepan of barely simmering water. Cook, stirring, until the mixture has melted and reached about 104°F (40°C). Remove the bowl from the saucepan and stir in the feuilletine flakes. Spread into a thin layer (about ⅒ inch/3 mm) over the Joconde sponge disk. Place in the refrigerator for at least 10 minutes or until using.

Spiced cream

01. In a small bowl, dissolve the gelatin powder in the 122°F (50°C) water. Using the mortar and pestle, lightly crush the cardamom pods, cloves, and cinnamon stick. Place the spices in a small saucepan with the 65 g water and bring to a boil. Remove from the heat and stir in the Earl Grey tea, then cover and let infuse for 5 minutes. Strain through a fine-mesh sieve into a bowl.

02. Place 55 g of the spice-infused water in a small saucepan, add the cream and honey, and bring to a boil. In a small bowl, whisk together the egg yolk and sugar. Whisking continuously, gradually pour one-third of the hot liquid into the egg yolk mixture, then pour everything back into the saucepan. Stirring nonstop with a flexible spatula, cook over medium heat until the mixture reaches 172°F (78°C), then remove it from the heat and stir in the dissolved gelatin. Strain through a fine-mesh sieve into a bowl.

03. Place the chocolate in a bowl and pour half of the spice-infused mixture over it. Whisk until smooth. Pour in the rest in two equal quantities and whisk until smooth after each addition. Let thicken slightly. Cut a strip 18½ inches (47 cm) long from the acetate roll and use it to line the inside of the 6-inch (15-cm) tart ring. Set the ring on a baking sheet lined with a guitar sheet and pour 200 g of the spiced cream into the ring. Place the baking sheet in the freezer for 1 hour, or until the cream is frozen.

→

SPICED CREAM

2 G   *gelatin powder*
10 G   *water, heated to 122°F (50°C)*
1 G   *green cardamom pods*
1 G   *whole cloves*
1 G   *cinnamon stick*
65 G   *water*
2 G   *loose-leaf Earl Grey tea*
55 G   *heavy cream*
7 G   *fir or pine honey*
20 G   *egg yolk (1 yolk from 1 large egg)*
8 G   *demerara sugar*
65 G   *Valrhona Jivara milk chocolate, 40% cacao, chopped*

—

MANDARIN CONFIT

100 G   *peeled mandarin (about 2 small mandarins)*
60 G   *superfine sugar*

—

SPICED GANACHE

1 G   *green cardamom pods*
1 G   *whole cloves*
2 G   *cinnamon stick*
90 G   *heavy cream*
8 G   *fir or pine honey*
60 G   *Valrhona Jivara milk chocolate, 40% cacao, chopped*
40 G   *Valrhona Extra Bitter dark chocolate, 61% cacao, chopped*

—

CHOCOLATE-CARAMEL MOUSSE

45 G   *superfine sugar*
95 G   *heavy cream*
120 G   *Valrhona Guanaja dark chocolate, 70% cacao, chopped*
40 G   *egg yolks (2 yolks from large eggs)*
25 G   *demerara sugar*
225 G   *heavy cream, whipped to soft peaks*

—

   velvet coating (OPTIONAL, SEE NOTES)
50 G   *cocoa butter*
100 G   *Valrhona Extra Bitter dark chocolate, 61% cacao, chopped*

—

DECORATION

   matcha powder
1   *star anise pod*
1/2   *cinnamon stick*
1   *whole clove*
1   *green cardamom pod about 20 fresh thyme sprigs, large and small*

Mandarin confit

01.   Separate the mandarin into segments and cut each segment into ¼-inch (5-mm) pieces. Place the pieces in a small saucepan with the sugar and stir carefully to distribute the sugar evenly without crushing the fruit. Let macerate at room temperature for 2 hours.

02.   Bring the mandarin-sugar mixture to a boil. If you have a refractometer, use it to check the sugar content. Continue to cook until the mixture reaches 40° to 45° Brix. If you do not have a refractometer, let the mixture cook at a boil for 2 to 3 minutes. Transfer to a bowl, press plastic wrap over the surface, and let cool in the refrigerator.

03.   Once the confit has cooled completely, transfer it to a pastry bag and pipe 80 of confit over the frozen spiced cream, making a ring shape. Return the baking sheet to the freezer.

Spiced ganache

01.   Using the mortar and pestle, lightly crush the cardamom pods, cloves, and cinnamon stick. Place the spices in a saucepan with the cream and honey and bring to a boil, then remove from the heat and let infuse for 10 minutes.

02.   Place both chocolates in a medium bowl. Strain the spice-infused cream into a clean saucepan and return it to a boil. Pour half of the spice-infused mixture over the chocolate and whisk until smooth. Pour in the rest in two equal quantities and whisk until smooth after each addition.

03.   Pour the ganache over the spiced cream and mandarin confit in the tart ring and return to the freezer for at least 1 hour, or until set. Remove the tart ring and acetate strip, then return the component to the freezer for 2 hours, or until frozen.

Chocolate-caramel mousse

01.   In a small heavy saucepan, heat the superfine sugar until it melts and begins to caramelize. Gently swirl the pan. As soon as fine bubbles appear on the surface, remove the pan from the heat and pour in the cream. Stir to combine and bring to a boil.

02.   Place the chocolate in a large bowl. In a separate bowl, whisk together the egg yolks and demerara sugar. Whisking continuously, gradually pour one-third of the hot cream mixture into the egg yolk mixture. Pour back into the saucepan, whisking continuously. Still whisking, cook over medium heat until the custard reaches 172°F (78°C).

03.   Strain through a fine-mesh sieve into the bowl with the chocolate. Whisk until smooth, then fold in the whipped cream. Transfer the mousse to a pastry bag fitted with the ½-inch (12-mm) plain tip.

04.   Set the 7-inch (18-cm) tart ring on a baking sheet lined with a guitar sheet and place the 6-inch (15-cm) round frozen component in the center of the ring. Pipe mousse around the frozen component to fill the space in the ring completely, making sure there are no air pockets, then cover with a thin layer of mousse and smooth it over well.

05.   Place the Joconde sponge disk on top with the feuilletine layer facing down. Freeze for at least 2 hours, or until frozen.

Velvet coating and decoration

01.   If you have a chocolate spray gun, prepare the velvet coating: place the cocoa butter and white chocolate together in a medium bowl set over a saucepan of barely simmering water. Cook, stirring, until the mixture has melted and reached about 104°F (40°C). Transfer to the spray gun. Remove the frozen component from the freezer, warm the ring slightly with your hands, and remove it. Immediately spray the sides evenly with the velvet coating.

02.   Dust the sides of the gâteau irregularly with matcha powder to create the illusion of lichen on a tree. Draw lines on the top to resemble tree rings. Place 1 star anise pod and ½ cinnamon stick on top and arrange 1 clove and 1 cardamom pod around them. Stick the thyme sprigs into the top and sides, as if they had sprouted out of the stump.

NOTES: Be sure to use the best, freshest spices you can find. We often pay less attention to the dry ingredients, but, in reality, the flavor of this gâteau hinges on the quality of the spices.

We use a custom mold to get the authentic tree trunk shape. Using tart rings is a way to approximate the shape at home.

If you do not have a chocolate spray gun, you can use unsweetened cocoa powder instead. First, thaw the cake in the refrigerator for at least 4 hours, then dust the sides evenly with cocoa powder before serving.

Amourissime

ACTIVE TIME	RESTING TIME	COOKING TIME
1 hour 30 minutes	*7 hours*	*20 minutes*

One day, I felt like creating a rose cake, and Valentine's Day was the perfect excuse to make a sweet that celebrates love. In this recipe, I combine rose with red currants. This fruit links the chocolate and rose flavors and makes the rose aroma linger.

Makes 6

EQUIPMENT

1	*22 × 14-inch (56 × 36-cm) pastry frame*
1	*instant-read thermometer*
1	*stand mixer + 2 mixer bowls*
1	*silicone mold with 1½-inch (4-cm) half-sphere cavities*
1	*refractometer (optional)*
2	*pastry bags*
1	*Silikomart SF186 silicone mold with heart-shaped cavities*

—

ALMOND JOCONDE SPONGE

280 G	*lightly beaten eggs (about 5½ large eggs), at room temperature*
275 G	*egg whites (about 9 whites from large eggs), at room temperature and divided*
375 G	*almond flour*
230 G	*confectioners' sugar*
185 G	*unsalted butter*
72 G	*pastry flour (T45)*
85 G	*superfine sugar*

—

FEUILLETINE LAYER

40 G	*almond praline paste*
15 G	*Valrhona Jivara milk chocolate, 40% cacao, chopped*
10 G	*Valrhona Extra Bitter dark chocolate, 61% cacao, chopped*
40 G	*feuilletine flakes*

→

Almond Joconde sponge

01.   Preheat the oven to 340°F (170°C) and place the pastry frame on a baking sheet lined with parchment paper. Whisk together the eggs and 125 g of the egg whites (about 4 whites) in a large bowl set over a saucepan of barely simmering water. Whisking, heat the eggs to about 104°F (40°C). Transfer to one of the stand mixer bowls and fit the mixer with the whisk attachment. Sift in the almond flour and confectioners' sugar together, then beat on high speed until the mixture is pale and thick.

02.   Melt the butter to 122°F (50°C) in a large bowl set over a saucepan of barely simmering water. Remove from the heat and whisk in one-fourth of the beaten egg mixture until emulsified. Sift the pastry flour into the mixer bowl with the rest of the egg mixture and gently fold it in.

03.   Combine the remaining 150 g egg whites with the superfine sugar in the second mixer bowl and beat until the whites hold firm peaks.

04.   Using a flexible spatula, gently fold the whites into the egg and flour mixture until only a few white streaks remain, then fold in the butter mixture until well blended.

05.   Pour the batter into the pastry frame and smooth it into an even layer using an offset spatula. Bake for 20 minutes.

06.   Gently slide a spatula between the frame and the sponge to remove the frame. Then, carefully transfer the sponge to a rack and let it cool.

07.   Once the sponge has cooled completely, cut out six hearts the same size as the heart mold cavities.

Feuilletine layer

01.   Place the praline paste and both chocolates in a small bowl set over a saucepan of barely simmering water. Cook, stirring, until the mixture has melted and reached about 104°F (40°C). Remove the bowl from the saucepan and stir in the feuilletine flakes. Spread a thin layer of the mixture (about ⅒ inch/3 mm) over the Joconde sponge hearts. Place in the refrigerator for at least 10 minutes or until using.

Red currant-rose cream

01.   In a small bowl, dissolve the gelatin powder in the 122°F (50°C) water. In a large saucepan, bring the red currant purée to a boil. Meanwhile, in a separate small bowl, whisk together the sugar and cornstarch. In a large bowl, whisk together the eggs and egg yolks, then whisk in the sugar-cornstarch mixture. Whisking continuously, gradually pour one-third of the hot purée into the egg mixture. Pour back into the saucepan, whisking continuously. Still whisking, cook over medium heat until the mixture thickens and reaches 172°F (78°C), then remove it from the heat and stir in the butter, followed by the dissolved gelatin.

02.   Stir the mixture until well blended, then strain it through a fine-mesh sieve into a bowl and set it over a larger bowl filled with ice water to cool it quickly. Leave the bowl over ice water, stirring often, until the mixture thickens and reaches 41°F (5°C).

03.   Stir in the rose water until evenly distributed. Spoon 16 g of the red currant-rose cream into each of six cavities of the half-sphere mold. Place in the freezer for 2 hours, or until the cream is frozen.

→

RED CURRANT-ROSE CREAM

2 G *gelatin powder*
10 G *water, heated to 122°F (50°C)*
190 G *red currant purée*
120 G *superfine sugar*
12 G *cornstarch*
105 G *lightly beaten eggs (about 2 large eggs)*
95 G *egg yolks (about 5 yolks from large eggs)*
105 G *unsalted butter, at room temperature*
1.5 G *rose water*

—

RASPBERRY JAM

2 G *pectin NH*
65 G *superfine sugar, divided*
100 G *fresh raspberries*
15 G *glucose syrup*
6 G *freshly squeezed lemon juice*

—

CHOCOLATE-CARAMEL MOUSSE

30 G *superfine sugar*
55 G *heavy cream*
70 G *Valrhona Tulakalum dark chocolate, 75% cacao (SEE NOTES), chopped*
25 G *egg yolks (about 1 yolk from 1 large egg)*
15 G *demerara sugar*
130 G *heavy cream, whipped to soft peaks*

—

DARK CHOCOLATE GLAZE

7 G *gelatin powder*
35 G *water, heated to 122°F (50°C)*
95 G *superfine sugar*
50 G *unsweetened cocoa powder*
60 G *heavy cream*
130 G *water*
25 G *invert sugar (Trimoline)*

—

DECORATION

Valrhona dark chocolate pearls
fresh rose petals
fresh red currants

Raspberry jam

01. Combine the pectin and 15 g of the sugar in a small bowl. In a small saucepan, combine the remaining 50 g sugar with the raspberries, glucose, and lemon juice and cook over medium heat, stirring often. If you have a refractometer, use it to check the sugar content. Continue to cook until the mixture reaches 56 °Brix. If you do not have a refractometer, let the mixture cook at a boil for 3 minutes. Whisk in the pectin-sugar mixture and cook over medium heat, whisking continuously, for 30 seconds to activate the pectin, allowing it to firm up.

02. Transfer the jam to a bowl, press plastic wrap over the surface, and place in the refrigerator to cool. When the jam has cooled completely, transfer it to a pastry bag. Remove the half-sphere mold from the freezer and pipe raspberry jam over the red currant-rose cream, filling the six cavities completely. Return the mold to the freezer for 2 hours, or until the jam has frozen.

Chocolate-caramel mousse

01. In a small heavy saucepan, heat the superfine sugar over low to medium heat until it melts and begins to caramelize. Gently swirl the pan. As soon as fine bubbles appear on the surface, remove the pan from the heat and pour in the cream. Stir to combine and bring to a boil.

02. Place the chocolate in a large bowl. In a separate medium bowl, whisk together the egg yolks and demerara sugar. Whisking continuously, gradually pour one-third of the hot cream mixture into the egg yolk mixture. Pour back into the saucepan, whisking continuously. Still whisking, cook over medium heat until the custard reaches 172°F (78°C).

03. Strain the custard through a fine-mesh sieve into the bowl with the chocolate. Whisk until smooth, then fold in the whipped cream. Transfer to the mousse to a pastry bag.

04. Pipe mousse into six cavities of the heart mold, filling them three-quarters full and taking care not to let any air enter. Remove the half-sphere mold from the freezer, turn out the frozen components, and nestle them into the center of the mousse in each cavity. Cover with mousse. Run a spatula over the top to smooth it and remove any excess mousse, then place the Joconde sponge hearts on top with the feuilletine layer facing down. Freeze for at least 3 hours.

Dark chocolate glaze and decoration

01. In a small bowl, dissolve the gelatin powder in the 122°F (50°C) water. In a separate small bowl, combine the superfine sugar and cocoa powder. Combine the cream, water, and invert sugar in a medium saucepan and bring to a boil over medium heat. Stirring continuously, gradually add the sugar-cocoa mixture to the saucepan. Maintain a boil over medium heat, stirring nonstop until the cocoa powder has dissolved completely, and the glaze is smooth and glossy. Stir in the dissolved gelatin. Strain the glaze through a fine-mesh sieve into a clean bowl, press plastic wrap over the surface, and let cool to 95°F (35°C).

02. When the glaze reaches 95°F (35°C), remove the heart mold from the freezer and turn the frozen hearts out onto a rack. Pour the glaze over them, ensuring they are well coated. Right before serving, arrange chocolate pearls around the bases and decorate the tops with fresh red currants and rose petals. Let thaw before serving.

NOTES: If you cannot find Valrhona Tulakalum chocolate for the mousse, look for another fruity dark chocolate with acidic notes reminiscent of the berries.

65 avenue de Breteuil, Paris 7th Arrondissement

Base
Recipes

Pastry Cream

ACTIVE TIME
30 minutes

Pastry cream is the foundation of Western pastry making. In Japan, the traditional equivalent is anko,
*or red bean paste. An essential component of many French pastries—including éclairs, réligieuses, and
Tropéziennes—pastry cream is also a key ingredient in other classic creams, such as frangipane and mousseline.
It is crucial to pay close attention to the cooking times.*

*Although most professional pastry kitchens have a dedicated machine for making pastry cream, I continue
to prepare it by hand, over a gas burner, not an electric one, because it is the very heart of our craft.*

Makes 800 g

EQUIPMENT

1	*large round-bottomed mixing bowl (cul-de-poule)*
1	*whisk*
1	*large saucepan*
—	
90 G	*egg yolks (about 4½ yolks from large eggs)*
125 G	*superfine sugar*
23 G	*pastry flour (T45)*
23 G	*cornstarch*
500 G	*whole milk*
¼	*vanilla bean, split lengthwise*
40 G	*unsalted butter, at room temperature*

Pastry cream

01.   Whisk the egg yolks in the round-bottomed bowl.

02.   Add the sugar and whisk until the mixture thickens slightly.

03.   Sift in the flour and cornstarch and gently whisk until combined.

05.   Pour the milk into the large saucepan. Scrape in the vanilla bean seeds and drop in the pod. Bring to a boil.

06.   Whisking continuously, gradually pour one-third of the hot milk into the egg yolk mixture. Whisk until smooth.

07.   Pour back into the saucepan and cook over high heat, whisking constantly to prevent the cream from sticking to the bottom of the pan. Cook until the cream thickens. When it is firm and smooth, remove the saucepan from the heat.

08.   Whisk in the butter.

09.   Pass the cream through a fine-mesh sieve into a baking dish.

10.   Press plastic wrap over the surface of the cream to prevent a skin from forming.

11.   Set the dish over ice water to quickly cool the pastry cream and prevent harmful bacteria from developing. Keep the pastry cream in the refrigerator for up to 24 hours.

Choux Pastry

ACTIVE TIME
20 minutes

*Classic choux pastry recipes often call for adding the eggs in several batches, but here,
I add them all at once, which produces perfect results.*

Makes 855 g

EQUIPMENT

1	*large saucepan*
1	*stand mixer*
—	
150 G	*water*
150 G	*whole milk*
130 G	*unsalted butter*
5 G	*superfine sugar*
5 G	*fine sea salt*
180 G	*all-purpose flour (T55), sifted*
235 G	*lightly beaten eggs (about 5 large eggs), at cool room temperature (about 64°F/18°C)*

Choux pastry

01.   Combine the water, milk, butter, sugar, and salt in the large saucepan and bring to a boil.

02.   Fit the stand mixer with the whisk attachment and pour the hot liquid into the mixer bowl. Add all the flour at once and beat on medium speed for 3 minutes.

03.   With the mixer running on medium speed, add the eggs all at once.

04.   Continue to mix on medium speed until the dough is smooth and falls from the whisk in a thick ribbon. The choux pastry is now ready to be piped.

NOTES: To ensure successful results, it is best to make the amount indicated here. You can freeze any surplus choux pastry for another use, but before freezing, you'll need to pipe it out into the desired final shape, so decide which recipe(s) you'll be making in advance. For example, if you're planning to make éclairs, you'll need to pipe out éclair shapes before freezing.

Inverse Puff Pastry

ACTIVE TIME
45 minutes

RESTING TIME
12 hours + 5 hours

It is crucial to respect the resting times.
Placing the dough in the refrigerator not only chills it but is also necessary to allow the gluten to rest.
Patience is the key to success.

Makes 1.8 kg (see notes)

EQUIPMENT

1	*stand mixer*
2	*guitar sheets*
1	*rolling pin*
1	*instant-read thermometer*

—

BUTTER BLOCK

600 G	*unsalted European-style butter, preferably 84% fat (beurre sec), at room temperature*
240 G	*all-purpose flour (T55)*

—

BASE DOUGH (DÉTREMPE)

240 G	*unsalted butter*
180 G	*water, chilled to about 41°F (5°C)*
4 G	*white vinegar, chilled to about 41°F (5°C)*
565 G	*pastry flour (T45)*
11 G	*fine sea salt*

Butter block

01.　The day before laminating and baking the dough, fit the stand mixer with the dough hook and place the butter and flour in the bowl. Knead on medium speed until well blended and smooth.

02.　Turn the mixture out onto one of the guitar sheets. Using the rolling pin, shape it into a rough rectangle thin enough to fold, then trim the edges to make a perfectly rectangular block. Cover with plastic wrap and refrigerate for 12 hours.

Base dough (détrempe)

01.　The day before laminating and baking the dough, melt the 240 g butter to about 104°F (40°C) and let it cool to 86°F (30°C). In a bowl, combine the chilled water and vinegar.

02.　Place the flour and salt in the stand mixer bowl. Add the water-vinegar mixture and the 86°F (30°C) butter. Knead on medium speed for 5 to 10 minutes, until a smooth dough forms.

03.　Turn the dough out onto the second guitar sheet. Using the rolling pin, shape it into a rough rectangle. Keep rolling until it is the same size as the butter block. If needed, trim it to achieve a perfect rectangular shape. Cover the dough with plastic wrap and refrigerate it for 12 hours.

Laminating inverse puff pastry

SEE THE STEP-BY-STEP INSTRUCTIONS ON PAGES 174–175.

→

NOTES: Once you have completed the laminating process, you can divide this dough up into the amounts needed for each recipe. Any leftover dough can be frozen.

Step-by-Step

LAMINATING INVERSE PUFF PASTRY

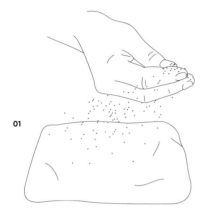

01

Remove the butter block from the refrigerator
and dust it with flour.

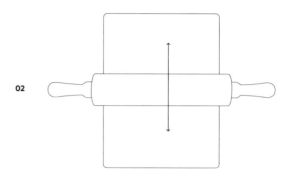

02

Roll it into a rectangle.

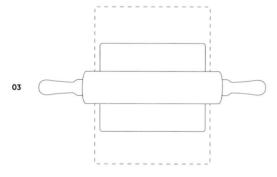

03

Do the same with the base dough (*détrempe*),
forming a rectangle about as wide as the
butter block but one-third shorter.

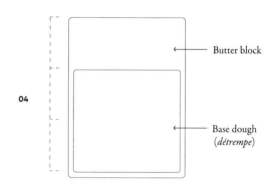

04

Butter block

Base dough
(*détrempe*)

Place the base dough rectangle over the butter block,
lining up the bottom edges.

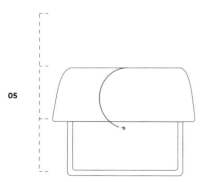

05

Fold the top part of the butter block over the base dough.

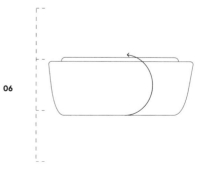

06

Fold the resulting rectangle in half.

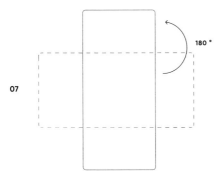

07

Give the dough a quarter turn to the left.

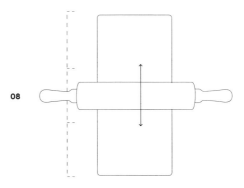

08

Roll the dough out lengthwise until it is
three times as long as it is wide.

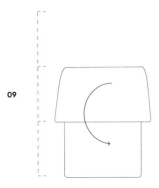

09

Fold one-third of the dough towards
you from the top, then fold the bottom
over the top, like folding a letter.

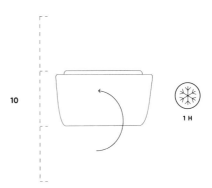

10

Cover the dough with plastic wrap
and refrigerate it for 1 hour.

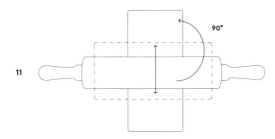

11

Position the dough so that a short edge is facing
you—the flap should be on the side. Roll it out again
until it is three times as long as it is wide. Again, fold
one-third of the dough towards you from the top and
fold the bottom over the top, like folding a letter.

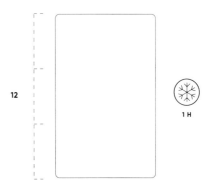

12

Cover the dough with plastic wrap and
refrigerate it for 1 hour. Repeat the same
rolling, folding, and chilling process twice
more. When you have finished, refrigerate the
dough for at least 1 hour before using it.

Sweet Shortcrust Pastry and Chocolate Sweet Shortcrust Pastry

ACTIVE TIME
30 minutes

RESTING TIME
3 hours

*Almond and hazelnut flour add depth of flavor to this pâte sucrée recipe.
But the amount used is small, so the taste is not overpowering.*

Makes 1 kg

EQUIPMENT

1   *stand mixer*

—

SWEET SHORTCRUST PASTRY

180 G   *confectioners' sugar*
4 G   *fine sea salt*
265 G   *unsalted butter, at room temperature*
85 G   *lightly beaten eggs (about 1¾ large eggs), at room temperature*
45 G   *almond flour*
24 G   *hazelnut flour*
400 G   *all-purpose flour (T55)*

—

CHOCOLATE SWEET
SHORTCRUST PASTRY

175 G   *confectioners' sugar*
4 G   *fine sea salt*
265 G   *unsalted butter, at room temperature*
85 G   *lightly beaten eggs (about 1¾ large eggs), at room temperature*
40 G   *almond flour*
24 G   *hazelnut flour*
360 G   *all-purpose flour (T55)*
40 G   *unsweetened cocoa powder*

Sweet shortcrust pastry

01.   Fit the stand mixer with the paddle attachment and add the confectioners' sugar, salt, and butter to the bowl. Beat on medium speed until smooth.

02.   With the mixer running on medium speed, gradually beat in the eggs. Sift the almond flour, hazelnut flour, and all-purpose flour together into the bowl, then beat on low speed until just incorporated.

03.   Cover the dough with plastic wrap and let it rest in the refrigerator for 3 hours before using.

Chocolate sweet shortcrust pastry

01.   Fit the stand mixer with the paddle attachment and add the confectioners' sugar, salt, and butter to the bowl. Beat on medium speed until smooth.

02.   With the mixer running on medium speed, gradually beat in the eggs. Sift the almond flour and hazelnut flour together into the bowl, then beat on low speed until just incorporated. Sift the all-purpose flour and cocoa powder together into the bowl and beat just until well blended and smooth.

03.   Cover the dough with plastic wrap and let it rest in the refrigerator for 3 hours before using.

Almond Cream

ACTIVE TIME
15 minutes

Almond cream is a staple of French pastry making.
When used in fruit tarts, it is typically spread across the base of the pastry shell and baked before being topped
with fresh fruit or whipped cream. It is also used in the Mont Blanc recipe, spread across the phyllo shell
before baking, and as a filling for the Lemon King Cake along with pastry cream.

Makes 770 g

EQUIPMENT

1	*stand mixer*
1	*large round-bottomed mixing bowl*
1	*instant-read thermometer*
—	
200 G	*confectioners' sugar*
200 G	*almond flour*
200 G	*unsalted butter, at room temperature*
170 G	*lightly beaten eggs (about 3½ large eggs)*

Almond cream

01.   Sift the confectioners' sugar and almond flour separately into two separate bowls.

02.   Fit the stand mixer with the paddle attachment and place the butter and confectioners' sugar in the bowl. Beat on low speed just until well combined, without incorporating too much air (see notes).

03.   Place the eggs in the round-bottomed mixing bowl and set over a saucepan of barely simmering water. Cook, stirring, until the eggs reach about 86°F (30°C). With the mixer running on low speed, gradually add the warmed eggs to the butter-sugar mixture, then incorporate the almond flour. Cover and store in the refrigerator for up to 24 hours.

NOTES: If you incorporate too much air into the butter and sugar mixture, the almond cream may expand and then collapse during baking.

Lining a Tart Ring with Phyllo Dough

ACTIVE TIME
10 minutes

Phyllo pastry lends tarts a unique texture that cannot be achieved with shortcrust or puff pastry. The dough is thin and supple, but by layering three sheets and brushing each with butter before baking, the results are crisp.

For the Mont Blanc

EQUIPMENT

1	*6-inch (15-cm) tart ring*

—

INGREDIENTS

60 G	*melted unsalted butter + more as needed*
3	*sheets phyllo dough*

For the Apple Mousse Tartlets

EQUIPMENT

10	*3-inch (8-cm) tart rings, ¾ inch (1.5 cm) deep*

—

INGREDIENTS

60 G	*melted unsalted butter + more as needed*
6	*sheets phyllo dough*

Folding the phyllo dough for the Apple Mousse Tartlets (p. 86) and the Mont Blanc (p. 140)

01.   Brush a thin layer of melted butter over one sheet of phyllo dough. Cover with a second sheet and brush with butter. Repeat with the third sheet.

02.   Smooth the top with your hand to remove any air.

03.   If you are making the Apple Mousse Tartlets, layer the 3 remaining sheets of phyllo dough in the same way, separately, so that you end up with two three-sheet stacks.

04.   If you are making the Mont Blanc, cut the dough into one 8-inch (20-cm) square. If you are making the Apple Mousse Tartlets, cut the dough into ten 4½-inch (11-cm) squares.

Lining a tart ring with phyllo dough

SEE THE STEP-BY-STEP INSTRUCTIONS ON PAGE 179.

$\longrightarrow$

Step-by-Step

LINING A TART RING WITH PHYLLO DOUGH

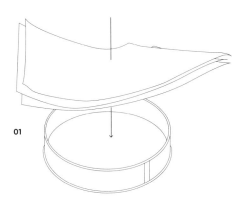

01

Lay the square of phyllo dough flat over the ring,
without pressing it down.

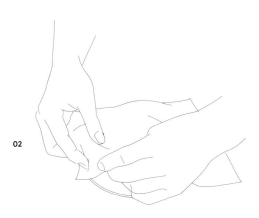

02

Turn the ring so that one corner of the dough square faces
you. The triangular corners overhanging the ring should
measure at least 2 inches (5 cm) from tip to base.

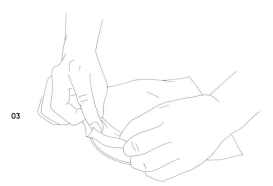

03

Pinch the base of the triangle opposite you to make a fold
that is just over ½ inch (1.5 cm) long.

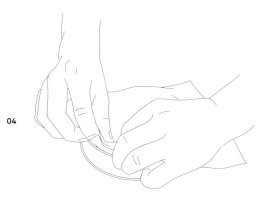

04

Tuck this fold inside the ring. The top edge
of the dough will stick out slightly.

05

Work your way around the ring from left to right,
repeating this folding and tucking process and
overlapping the folds as you go. When you reach
the second corner of the dough, do the same.

06

Continue until all the dough is inside the ring,
then fold down the corners and tuck in the tips
between the dough and the ring.

Tempering Chocolate

The goal of tempering is to stabilize the fat crystals in the cocoa butter as much as possible. This technical step is crucial to ensuring that the chocolate sets well and has a glossy sheen and snap. It also guarantees a melt-in-the-mouth consistency and prevents white splotches, known as bloom, from forming on the surface.

Tempering basics

Finicky by nature, cocoa butter is made up of six types of fat molecules, or crystals, which react differently depending on the melting temperature and their density and form. Because of this range of reactions, untempered chocolate does not keep as well and can have an unpleasant taste. Tempering stabilizes the different crystals and is essential for consistent, professional results.

Cocoa butter crystals are typically classified from Form I to Form VI. The higher the number, the higher their melting temperature.

Among these six molecules, Forms I to IV melt at relatively low temperatures and make chocolate difficult to unmold and unsuitable for pastry making.

Form VI has stable crystals, but because the melting temperature is high, bloom can occur in the transformation process. This chocolate does not melt in the mouth, and as the crystals are larger, their texture remains grainy and unappealing even when melted.

Form V is the crystal type most strived for in pastry making. It melts at 91°F (33°C), just slightly lower than human body temperature. Form V crystals are delicate and make the chocolate smooth and glossy with a brittle snap. The chocolate also contracts well when it sets, making it easy to unmold.

There are three main ways to temper chocolate to obtain Form V crystals. All three are suitable for the recipes in this book. These techniques are not very complicated, but they do require a little skill and an instant-read thermometer.

NOTES: The weights of the ingredients are not indicated here, as they can be found in the specific recipes in the book. The most important thing in tempering is to respect the precise temperatures indicated in each technique. These different techniques work with any amount of chocolate you are using.

Tabling (tempering on a marble slab)

01.   Melt the chocolate in a bowl set over a saucepan of barely simmering water, stirring regularly, until the temperature reaches 131°F (55°C) for dark chocolate and 113°F (45°C) for milk and white chocolate.

02.   Once the chocolate reaches this temperature, remove the bowl from the saucepan and pour two-thirds of the chocolate onto a marble slab. Using an offset spatula, spread the chocolate into a thin layer. Then, using a chocolate spatula or scraper, push the chocolate from the outside toward the center. Working quickly, repeat these spreading and gathering steps until the chocolate cools and begins to harden. Dark chocolate should reach 82°F (28°C), milk chocolate 81°F (27°C), and white chocolate 79°F (26°C).

03.   Return the chocolate on the slab to the bowl with the remaining chocolate and gently stir until the temperature reaches 88°F (31°C) for dark chocolate, 84°F (29°C) for milk chocolate, and 82°F (28°C) for white chocolate.

NOTES: These temperatures are general guidelines and may vary depending on the amount of cocoa butter in the chocolate. The higher the proportion of cocoa butter, the higher the tempering temperature. The tempering process may need to be adapted depending on the brand and type of chocolate.

Before starting, make sure the marble slab is clean, perfectly dry, and close to 73°F (23°C).

Tabling is a traditional technique. Spreading the chocolate across the marble cools it more quickly than with other methods. Working with a scraper while keeping an eye on the temperature allows you to observe and feel the changes that occur as the chocolate sets.

Tempering in a bowl

01.   Chop the chocolate finely and melt it in a bowl set over a saucepan of barely simmering water, stirring regularly, until the temperature reaches 131°F (55°C) for dark chocolate and 113°F (45°C) for milk and white chocolate.

02.   When the chocolate reaches this temperature, place the bowl in a larger bowl filled with cold water. Stir continuously until dark chocolate cools to 82°F (28°C), milk chocolate to 81°F (27°C), and white chocolate to 79°F (26°C).

03.   Return the bowl to the saucepan and stir gently until the temperature reaches 88°F (31°C) for dark chocolate, 84°F (29°C) for milk chocolate, and 82°F (28°C) for white chocolate.

NOTES: Place the chocolate in a large enough bowl to avoid getting water in it. If you use ice water for the cold-water bath, make sure there is not too much water. If the water rises higher than the chocolate, water droplets are likely to form inside the bowl, causing the chocolate to seize up.

Avoid drastic differences in temperature. Stirring constantly ensures that the chocolate exposed to cold attains quick and even cooling and crystal formation. Similarly, ensure that the water in the hot water bath is not too hot—if the chocolate gets hotter than 34°C (93°F), even the desired Form V crystals will melt. Do not leave the chocolate over the water bath for too long, and stir it continuously.

Tempering by seeding

01.   Finely chop the chocolate and melt two-thirds of it in a bowl set over a saucepan of barely simmering water, stirring regularly, until the temperature reaches 131°F (55°C) for dark chocolate and 113°F (45°C) for milk and white chocolate.

02.   Add the remaining third of the chocolate and gradually stir it into the bowl.

03.   Stir continuously until the chocolate reaches the desired temperature: 88°F (31°C) for dark chocolate, 84°F (29°C) for milk chocolate, and 82°F (28°C) for white chocolate.

NOTES: Chop the chocolate finely enough so that it melts more or less evenly.

If any unmelted bits remain after the chocolate has reached the desired temperature, return the bowl to the hot-water bath for a few seconds, stirring continuously. Do not let the chocolate exceed the following temperatures: 90°F (32°C) for dark chocolate, 86°F (30°C) for milk chocolate, or 84°F (29°C) for white chocolate. Repeat this step until all the chocolate has melted.

Index

GLOSSARY

B

- BASE DOUGH: A mixture of flour, salt, and water used as the base dough for puff pastry, before incorporating the butter.
- BEATING: Vigorously mixing ingredients or a batter, typically using a whisk, to incorporate air and alter the texture or volume.
- BLIND BAKING: Pre-baking a tart shell before adding a filling with a high moisture content or that does not need baking. The dough or pastry is typically pricked with a fork and covered with parchment paper, and often pie weights, to prevent it from puffing up too much during baking.
- BROWNED BUTTER: Sweet or salted butter melted and gently cooked until it is hazelnut-colored and nutty-smelling.
- BUTTER, 84% FAT: Also known as beurre de tourage, this butter used to make puff pastry contains less water than conventional butter, so it has a higher melting point and is easier to work with. It produces wonderfully flaky results and superior flavor. Cultured European-style butters with 84% fat are the best substitute.
- BUTTER, ROOM TEMPERATURE: Butter softened to room temperature until it has a smooth, creamy consistency. When a recipe calls for room-temperature butter, remove it from the refrigerator at least 30 minutes before starting.
- BUTTER BLOCK: Butter mixed with flour or cornstarch to make puff pastry.

C

- CARAMEL: Sugar cooked to between 340°F and 355°F (170°C–180°C).
- CHIMNEY: A hole bakers make in dough to allow steam to escape during baking.
- COATING: Evenly covering a preparation with a glaze, sauce, coulis, or cream.
- CRIMPING: Pinching the edges of an unbaked tart shell using your fingers or a pastry pincher or scoring dough edges together using the tip of a knife to seal them together.
- CRYSTALLIZATION: The stabilization of the cocoa butter crystals in chocolate produced by tempering, ensuring the chocolate has a glossy sheen and snap when it sets.

D

- DEFLATING: To flatten/push down on dough to expel any air and gases produced during fermentation. This helps to distribute the air more evenly in the dough, resulting in a more regular crumb.
- DEGREES BRIX: A unit for measuring the sweetness or sugar concentration in a syrup.
- DUSTING: Sprinkling a thin layer of flour on a work surface, greased pan, or dough to prevent sticking.

E

- EGG WASH: An egg-based mixture brushed over dough to encourage browning during baking.
- EMULSION: A smooth blend of two or more liquids that do not usually mix together.

F

- FINE-MESH SIEVE: Also known as a fine-mesh strainer or chinois, depending on the shape, this is an essential tool for filtering mixtures containing impurities or seeds to obtain perfectly smooth results.
- FOLDING IN: The process of gently blending a light and airy mixture into a denser one or vice versa using a lifting and turning movement, typically with a flexible spatula, while turning the bowl. As opposed to stirring or beating, folding in retains as much air as possible and prevents the mixture from deflating.
- FROTHY: The consistency of a mixture that is being beaten or whisked when it forms air bubbles and begins to thicken and cling to the whisk.

G

- GANACHE: a mixture of melted chocolate, cream, milk and room-temperature butter used to fill or coat pastries.
- GLAZE: A smooth, shiny layer coating cakes and other pastries, often poured warm over cakes while they are frozen.
- GREASING: Coating the inside of a cake pan with a thin layer of fat, typically room-temperature butter.
- GUITAR SHEETS: Food-safe plastic sheets that are sturdier than regular plastic wrap and parchment paper but less rigid than acetate. They make it easy to unmold pastry components and guarantee a smooth surface. When tempered chocolate sets on guitar sheets, it develops a glossy sheen.

I

- INCORPORATING: Adding one or more ingredients to a mixture and stirring or mixing until evenly distributed.
- INVERT SUGAR (TRIMOLINE®): Also known as invert sugar syrup, this is a viscous syrup made of glucose and fructose. It helps retain moisture in baked goods and produces a smoother texture in ganache and ice cream.

K

- KNEADING: Working dough with your hands or a mixer fitted with a dough hook to combine the ingredients and develop the gluten network.

L

- LAMINATING: The process of folding and rolling butter into dough to make puff pastry. Produces thin, alternating layers, resulting in light, flaky pastries.
- LINING: Gently fitting rolled-out dough into tart rings or cake pans.

M

- MACARONNAGE: The French term for folding macaron batter using a flexible spatula to obtain perfectly smooth macaron shells.
- MEASUREMENTS: Because of the precise nature of this book, only metric weights have been provided. To ensure the best results, weigh your ingredients using a digital scale.
- MIRROR GLAZE: A clear reflective glaze used by pastry chefs to create a protective glossy sheen. Available in specialty shops.

P

- PECTIN NH: A thermally reversible pectin that can be melted and reset as needed.
- PIPING: Using a pastry bag, often fitted with a pastry tip, to control the flow and shape of batters, doughs, and creams.
- PRICKING: Poking holes in rolled-out dough using the tines of a fork to prevent the dough from puffing up too much during baking.

R

- REFRACTOMETER: A tool used to measure the degrees Brix (°Brix), or sugar content, in a syrup. While not essential, it does help to obtain the ideal level of sweetness and ensure consistent results.
- RIBBON: Said of a mixture that is thick enough to fall off a spatula or whisk in thick ribbons and lingers briefly on the surface before sinking back into the batter.
- ROLLING OUT: The process of rolling out dough to the desired thickness on a lightly floured surface using a rolling pin.
- ROUND-BOTTOMED MIXING BOWL: A light stainless-steel bowl with a rounded bottom used for mixing ingredients and for heating them over a hot water bath (bain-marie).

S

- SABLER: The French verb for mixing fat (typically butter) with flour to obtain a dough with a crumbly, sand-like texture.
- SEAM: The place where the dough edges meet after shaping.
- SHAPING: Forming dough into a desired shape using your hands.
- SIFTING: Passing flour or another dry ingredient through a fine-mesh sieve to aerate it and remove impurities and clumps.

- SNOW SUGAR: A non-melting sugar that looks like confectioners' sugar but does not dissolve on moist cakes or tarts.
- SOAKING (IMBIBER): Brushing or pouring a syrup over a cake to flavor and/or moisten and soften it.

T

- TEMPERING: The process of melting chocolate, cooling it, and reheating it to a given temperature to stabilize the fat crystals in the cocoa butter.
- TURNING: Folding a piece of dough into three or four during the laminating process.

W

- WATER BATH: A method for gently heating mixtures that can separate or burn easily. A stovetop water bath consists of a bowl set over a saucepan of barely simmering water. In the oven, water baths prevent egg-based preparations such as custards and cheesecakes from curdling or drying out. In this case, custard-filled ramekins or pans are placed in a high-sided baking dish and very hot water is poured in until it reaches halfway up the sides.
- WHISKING OR WHIPPING: (1) Mixing the various components of a recipe using a whisk (either handheld or the whisk attachment on a stand mixer); (2) whisking a mixture to incorporate air and add volume.

Z

- ZESTING: Removing the zest from a citrus fruit, avoiding the bitter white pith. To obtain finely grated zest, use a Microplane grater or the fine holes of a box grater.

Mori Yoshida's Career

The son of a talented pastry chef in Shimizu, in the Shizuoka region, located three hours from Tokyo,
Morihide grew up steeped in the world of his father's workshop, which produced both Japanese and Western pastries.
With such a family heritage, he seemed destined to follow in his father's footsteps.

However, as a young man, Mori did not imagine himself becoming a pastry chef, even though he admits to having a very sharp palate—he can distinguish between the different fats in fish and appreciate the subtle changes in the way strawberries taste as the season progresses.

The pursuit of taste has always fascinated him. But his decision to attend a pastry school in Tokyo after high school was motivated primarily by a desire to live in the capital city; he hoped to realize his dream of becoming an actor. He seemed a poor student compared to his classmates, most of whom were the sons and daughters of pastry chefs, destined to take over the family business. He preferred to spend his time daydreaming and exploring the city.

What bothered him about being a pastry chef was that his future seemed to have been decided for him: he would help his father bake cakes, take over the household, settle in his hometown forever, and lead a predictable life. Even an internship in France, in Chinon, failed to excite him. He had exceptional tasting skills, but missed out on the magic of pastry that would later fascinate him.

So, how did this jaded young man become a pastry chef who now retreats to his workshop from morning till night? The answer surely lies in his desire to take on challenges, a force that has always driven him.

2000: Tokyo debut

With his pastry diploma in hand, Mori got his start at Tokyo's Park Hyatt hotel, as part of the spirited brigade of pastry chefs who regularly take part in the Coupe du Monde de la Pâtisserie and other prestigious competitions.
The day-to-day work was a real challenge. Chefs had to make desserts and pastries for the hotel's restaurants and its boutique, in addition to brunch and special orders. In the kitchen, everyone bustled about, hastening to respond to a wide variety of requests, such as inventing a dessert for a truffle-only dinner, or creating a cake to round off a typically Japanese meal.

Despite the hectic pace, Mori has nothing but fond memories of this period. Pastry chef Yokota, who introduced Mori to the profession and placed his trust in him, helped the young man find his vocation. Mori has great admiration for his mentor. It was this initial experience that forged Mori's pastry-making philosophy: work as part of a team rather than alone, and seek out flavors that are accessible to all, rather than personal "creations." It was here that he learned "what is good."

2005: first pâtisserie in Shizuoka

Mori was working in the pâtisserie-teahouse that chef Yokota had opened in Saitama when fate threw him a new challenge.

At the request of his father, who was not in the best of health, Mori decided to return to Shizuoka to take over the family business. In 2005, he opened his own boutique, Pâtisserie Naturelle Nature & Co.

But the beginning proved difficult. His cakes did not easily win fans among his father's clientele. To make his mark, he decided to take part in the Coupe du Monde de la Pâtisserie, a program broadcast by Tokyo Television. It was 2006, and the young chef was twenty-nine years old. The competition awakened his fighting spirit. He won the championship with a Mont Blanc in seven shades of brown. The very next day, customers were lined up outside his store to buy the new champion's cakes. And the day after that—his life had taken a new turn.

2008: a discovery that changes everything

But becoming a famous pastry chef in his region was not enough for Mori. Once again, he saw his future unfold before him: he would open a second pâtisserie in a department store, buy a nice car, and get bored. On a trip to France, Mori was struck by the flavors of French pastry, which he was only just discovering.

It was a revelation. He realized that in Japan, the flour was not of the same quality, the butter had a different aroma, and the fruit was not as flavorful. On top of that, Japan's humid climate softened macarons and puff pastry. What was the point of continuing to make "Western-style" cakes, while pretending he had never tasted the real thing? From then on, Mori had only one goal: to move to France and take the risk of starting all over again.

2010: arrival in Paris

As soon as he arrived in Paris, Mori enrolled in French classes and undertook a series of internships at Guy Savoy, La Pâtisserie des Rêves, and Jacques Genin, while looking for a location for his own business. He found something he liked in the 7th Arrondissement, a neighborhood that his French acquaintances had advised against because it was quiet, and too far from the city center.

However, he thought the location was perfect to set up shop and build a loyal following of customers with discerning palates.

In 2013, his dream finally came true in the form of the MORI YOSHIDA pâtisserie, at 65 Avenue de Breteuil. The simple, uncluttered boutique showcases his formidable talent for offering the great classics of French pâtisserie to an eager audience. His friends would later realize that Mori's intuition had been right.

2018: best professional pastry chef

But how do you spread the word about a shop in a residential area, run by a little-known Japanese pastry chef? Mori, who thrives on a challenge, tried for the second time in his life to find a solution: he took part in the television show Le Meilleur Pâtissier–Les Professionnels (The Best Pastry Chef—Professionals). The jurors were Pierre Hermé, Philippe Conticini, and Cyril Lignac. This time he was competing in France against French candidates who grew up working with flour and butter.

But he this new challenge did not frighten him: quite the contrary. The rest is history: Mori won the title of Best Professional Pastry Chef in 2018 and 2019, and success followed soon after.

2022: sharing and teaching

Today, Mori Yoshida has a solid reputation as a pastry chef who excels in the great classics. At first glance, his career appears to be a flawless "success story," which he immediately denies. He jokingly recalls that he went through a long "dark period," when nothing sold. But he never wanted to give in to the pressure to simply make "Japanese-style" cakes. If he had to compromise, why come to France in the first place? He could have just stayed Japan.

Mori does not see success as a goal in itself; it is first and foremost a way to make his voice heard. With his love of traditional pâtisserie, he wants most of all to pursue his life's quest: to find the "beautiful formulas" of French pâtisserie classics, to borrow an expression used by mathematicians, who describe good formulas as "beautiful."

To achieve this, media coverage is essential, so that people cannot say that he will never be able to achieve the quintessence of French pâtisserie because of his origins. Mori, as a Japanese pastry chef, would like most of all to pass on the flavors of authentic pâtisserie as one would a cultural heritage.

This book is the fourth challenge he has accepted. It brings together the recipes that have emerged from his love and appreciation for French pastry. Mori by no means considers them perfect, simply the best "for now"—his quest is ongoing.

This is why he goes to his workshop every morning, to continue kneading dough, tempering chocolate, and preparing croissants—because that is what a true pastry chef does.

Acknowledgments

It all began the day I told Julie Mathieu and Muriel Tallandier that
I wanted to leave a trace of my career.

I am infinitely grateful to them for listening to me and giving me so much invaluable
advice. I have been surrounded by a wonderful team who have enabled me to put down
on paper everything that is important to me about pastry making.
It is these people who enable me to go ever further, beyond what is "good."

I am so delighted to hold in my hands a book that exceeds my every expectation,
and I hope that, thanks to this collective work, cakes the world
over will be even more delicious.

—

Once again, I would like to thank all those who made
this project possible.

Julie Mathieu, Muriel Tallandier, Ryoko Sekiguchi, Emmanuel Le Vallois,
Benoit Berger, Caroline Faccioli, Faris Issad, Eugénie Pont, Sabine Houplain,
Élodie Rambaud, Akane Yorozu, Emiko Watanabe

The team at Mori Yoshida
The team at Éditions du Chêne

Masami Yoshida, Anna and Yugo and Léon,
Hiroo and Hatsuyo Yoshida, Shoji and Noriko Toya, Sato and Hisae Yoshida,
Kenichi and Mizuki Yoshida, Daisuke Sato

Hideo Yokota
Pierre Hermé

Shigeru Nojima
Masafumi Asakura

—

Finally, I would like to thank everyone who has helped make me who I am today.
I will try to do my very best and continue to create ever more delightful cakes.

Mori Yoshida

Gateaux: Sweets was first published in the United States
by Tra Publishing in 2025.

First published in 2022 by Éditions du Chêne–Hachette Livre
www.editionsduchene.fr

U.S. EDITION:
Text copyright by Mori Yoshida 2025
Photography copyright by Caroline Faccioli 2025
Illustration copyright by Derudderdesign

U.S. EDITION TEAM:
Publisher and Creative Director: Ilona Oppenheim
Art Director: Jefferson Quintana
Editorial Director: Lisa McGuinness
Publishing Coordinator: Jessica Faroy
Typesetter: Morgane Leoni
Translation: Ansley Evans and Kate Robinson
Copy editing: Carey Jones

This product is made of FSC®-certified and other controlled
material. Tra Publishing is committed to sustainability
in its materials and practices.

FSC
www.fsc.org
MIX
Paper | Supporting
responsible forestry
FSC® C019910

Printed and bound in China
by Artron Art Co., Ltd.

ISBN: 9781962098120

Tra Publishing
245 NE 37th Street
Miami, FL 33137
trapublishing.com

T tra.publishing

1 2 3 4 5 6 7 8 9 10

All photographs by Caroline Faccioli except:

© Unsplash/Behzad Ghaffarian: 12, 82.
© Unsplash/Clarisse Croset: 112;
© Unsplash/Grégoire Jeanneau: 138;
© Unsplash/Veronika Jorjobert: 38.